HOW TO
Prepare Your Curriculum Vitae

Revised Edition

Acy L. Jackson and C. Kathleen Geckeis

VGM Career Books

Chicago   New York   San Francisco   Lisbon   London   Madrid   Mexico City
Milan   New Delhi   San Juan   Seoul   Singapore   Sydney   Toronto

The McGraw-Hill Companies

Library of Congress Cataloging-in-Publication Data

Jackson, Acy L.
  How to prepare your curriculum vitae / Acy L. Jackson and C. Kathleen Geckeis.—Rev. ed.
      p.   cm.
  Rev. ed. of: How to prepare your curriculum vitae / Acy L. Jackson. 1998.
  Includes bibliographical references.
  ISBN 0-07-139044-8
  1. Résumés (Employment)   I. Geckeis, C. Kathleen.   II. Jackson, Acy L.   III. Title. How to prepare your curriculum vitae. 1998.

HF5383 .J24 2003
650.14'2—dc21   2002034314

1 2 3 4 5 6 7 8 9 0   QPD/QPD   2 1 0 9 8 7 6 5 4 3

ISBN 0-07-139044-8

McGraw-Hill books are available at special quantity discounts to use as premiums and sales promotions, or for use in corporate training programs. For more information, please write to the Director of Special Sales, Professional Publishing, McGraw-Hill, Two Penn Plaza, New York, NY 10121-2298. Or contact your local bookstore.

This book is printed on acid-free paper.

To my beloved grandchildren
Jamil Allette-Jackson
Lourdes Brontë Jackson
Quinn Sterling Julius Jackson
who constantly inspire me to excel in all my endeavors
—Acy L. Jackson

⟶⟳ ⟲⟵

To my parents
Jean and Roger Tucker
whose love and support sustain me in everything that I do
—C. Kathleen Geckeis

Contents

Acknowledgments

We wish to express our deepest appreciation to our esteemed colleagues and friends, who advised and encouraged us as we prepared this edition of *How to Prepare Your Curriculum Vitae*.

With gratitude, we thank Gerry Bazer, Dean of Arts and Sciences at Owens Community College, Toledo, Ohio, for his support and encouragement throughout this project. We are also appreciative of Deborah Wingert, Research Librarian at Terra Community College, Fremont, Ohio, whose congeniality and knowledge of resources have been of infinite value to us.

In addition, we are indebted to Dr. Orlando Reyes-Cairo and Dr. Warren Dick for their valuable contributions to the new chapter, "International Curricula Vitae."

Finally, a heartfelt thank you to Robin Bliss-Atkins for typing the appendices, and our sincerest thanks to Denise Betts, our patient and supportive editor.

Getting Started

The curriculum vitae, commonly referred to as a CV, Vita, or Vitae, is a detailed biographical description of one's educational and work background. It differs from a résumé, a one-page description of one's work experience and educational background not only in length but also in detail. The origin of the term *curriculum vitae* is Latin and means "the course of one's life or career." As such, a CV includes detailed information regarding one's academic coursework, professional experience, publications, and so on.

The curriculum vitae, long in use among professionals in higher education, has gained currency among undergraduates applying for admission to graduate and professional schools, as well as among applicants for selected areas of employment such as those in research, teaching, and management. Moreover, because of the growing tendency to use brief application forms—often only two pages long—some graduate and professional programs actually encourage applicants to enclose a CV with their applications. For these reasons, the curriculum vitae is often referred to as an "academic résumé." We have included sample curricula vitae in Chapters 5, 6, and 7.

This book provides effective and timely guidelines for:

- Soon-to-be college graduates

- Continuing graduates

- Professionals who need to prepare a CV

- Professionals who need to update a CV

- Professionals planning a career transition

As a resource, this book is especially suited to the needs of faculty and staff who provide academic, personal, and career/vocational counseling to those who are preparing to write their CVs and are in need of guidance.

As you prepare your CV, it is important to use the critical-thinking skills you have learned as a result of your education or training. Few individuals realize that the critical-thinking skills they acquire as they pursue an academic degree are transferable to other aspects of their lives. Take the skill of analysis, for example. Upon graduation, one can assume that an individual has acquired analytical skills such as problem solving and decision making. The biology major, for example, will have honed analytical skills by studying courses in the discipline, performing experiments in the laboratory, writing reports based on observations, and using data to reconsider the conditions under which those observations occurred. These very skills are transferable as the biology graduate begins the process of writing a CV and reexamining his or her life and academic career. Use the exercises provided at the end of this chapter to examine your life and your academic career. As you do so, remember to examine specifically those academic skills that are transferable to other aspects of your life and career.

The Emotional Dimension

The process of writing a curriculum vitae can be an exhilarating experience because it generates a heightened degree of pride in your accomplishments as well as an increased awareness of your skills. Begin the process with enthusiasm and a desire to share information about yourself. If you approach this process with anxiety or uncertainty about its efficacy, writing a curriculum vitae will not be a pleasurable experience.

If you are like most individuals, you will probably experience a mixture of emotions ranging from nonchalance to denial of the need to prepare a CV. You will probably have emotional highs and lows that will affect every aspect of the work to be accomplished. It is essential to recognize that your feelings about yourself have much to do with the degree of confidence with which you approach and effectively complete this process. Therefore, a little emotional introspection may well be in order.

View the process of preparing an effective CV as more than merely recording your educational and work background. Instead, make it an intensely satisfying experience by critically reflecting upon your life. In this frame of mind, then, consider the following exercises as a means of developing an emotional and intellectual foundation that will take you on an investigative course in the preparation of your CV. Return to this chapter whenever you need support in this effort. Keep in mind, however, that revisions, additions, and clarifications will occur naturally as your work progresses.

On the following pages you will find exercises that will assist you in exploring the emotional dimension of preparing your curriculum vitae. Since preparing to write a CV must begin with emotional reflection, we highly recommend that you articulate those emotions in a effort to anchor them. As you do so, you will generate confidence and a frame of mind conducive to successfully creating an effective CV. To begin, find a quiet place and allow yourself sufficient time to reflect on the emotional and intellectual dimensions of preparing your CV. Use the space provided below each exercise to record your reactions.

1. Describe your feelings as you begin this process.

_____

_____

_____

_____

_____

_____

2. List your strengths and the context in which you displayed each strength.

_____

_____

_____

_____

_____

_____

3. It is essential that you confront any uneasiness, discomfort, or negative feelings you have about your educational background and work experience. Write these feelings down and then set them aside. Do not dwell on them.

_____

_____

_____

_____

_____

_____

4. Now, ask yourself why you are writing your curriculum vitae.

_____

_____

_____

_____

_____

_____

_____

Identifying Competencies and Skills

After you have explored the emotional dimension of preparing your CV, the next stage in creating an effective curriculum vitae involves delineating your competencies and skills. Competencies are what a person can do well. They include all the things that he or she has learned as a result of acquiring a skill through education, training, and experience. By the same token, a skill defines the level at which one can perform a competency. As individuals develop, they obtain credentials stating the competencies and skills they have acquired and the level of proficiency at which they can perform them. Credentials usually take the form of diplomas, degrees, licenses, certificates, and so on.[1]

---

[1]Appalachia Educational Laboratory, Inc. Career Decision-Making Program. *Career Planning and Decision-Making for College.* Bloomington, IL: McKnight Publishing Co., 1980.

It is not always easy to separate the competencies and skills that are the outcomes of life experiences from those that result from structured educational experiences. Most people would insist that life, as a learning experience, should be included in one's CV. The competencies and skills that you have learned as a result of formal education or training are not only transferable to other venues but are also valuable tools in developing an effective CV. Your academic advisor, professor, and/or mentor can assist you in making these connections. This chapter, therefore, encourages individuals, whose experiences allow for such distinctions, to include them (see Step II). It provides step-by-step procedures for identifying educational and noneducational competencies and skills that might be listed on your CV.

Step I: Identify Your Competencies

The following classifications are meant to encourage you to take inventory of your competencies and skills, as well as to present them as effectively as possible on your CV. No effort has been made to define each competency—that would be too restrictive—or to place values on any competency or skill or group of competencies or skills. You are expected instead to make broad assessments, or self-statements, at this stage of the process. Using the list below as a guide, write several self-statements that describe your competencies and skills. This list addresses perspective—that is, how one sees one's education and experience, or how one views what one knows. The broad categories of *intellectual disposition*—an innate inclination toward ways of processing knowledge and information—and *intellectual maturity*—the ability to think critically about information—will help you establish your competencies and skills.

Intellectual Disposition
Commitment
Creativity
Curiosity
Enthusiasm
Imagination
Predisposition
   for Discovery
Sympathy/Empathy

Intellectual Maturity
Analysis
Assimilation of
   Information
Communication
Conceptualization
Critical Judgment
Cultural Perspective
Decision Making

**Intellectual
Maturity** *continued*
Discrimination
Interpersonal
Nominalization
Problem Solving

The following examples will guide you in developing self-statements, the first step in delineating your competencies and skills. Examples A and B describe specific details that you might use to describe your own intellectual disposition and maturity.

Example A: sympathetic toward economically disadvantaged; imaginative in creating scenarios for social change; committed to community involvement in decision-making processes

Example B: committed to consensus in policy decisions; effective utilization of mathematical and quantitative reasoning in marketing strategies; enthusiastic development of profits; employment of state-of-the-art communication techniques to interpersonal interactions

On the next page, you will find a worksheet that you can use to record your own intellectual disposition and maturity self-statements.

Exercise for Step I

Intellectual Disposition and Maturity Self-Statements

1. _____
   _____
   _____
   _____
   _____
   _____

2. _____
   _____
   _____
   _____
   _____
   _____

3. _____
   _____
   _____
   _____
   _____

4. _____
   _____
   _____
   _____

5. _____
   _____
   _____
   _____
   _____

Step II: Identify Your Skills

Record your competencies and skills and their applications in the following exercise. Do not be concerned about the way they might appear on your CV; the objective here is to generate as much information about yourself as possible. Use the lists below as preliminary guidelines for delineating your competencies and skills. A *competency* can be defined as that which you know as a result of your education and training; it reflects content and knowledge. Competencies might include a specific body of knowledge—that is, boundaries that divide traditional disciplines. For example:

- Accounting

- Commmunication

- Economics

- Humanities

- Language

- Mathematics

- Natural Sciences

- Physical Sciences

- Quantitative Reasoning

- Social Sciences

Skills, on the other hand, reflect what you do with what you know, or the degree to which you perform a competency, a technique, or a craft. For example:

- Written/Spoken Language
  Precision
  Fluency
  Clarity
  Persuasion
  Concision

- Information Processing
  Select
  Interpret
  Store
  Place Information into a Larger Context

- Observation

- Research

- Analysis

- Organization

- Problem Solving

- Logical Reasoning

- Historical Method

- Scientific Method

- Stimulated Listening

- Rhetorical Style

- Evaluation

- Improvisation

- Conceptualization

- Counseling Theories

- Advising

- Decision Making

- Evaluation

- Negotiation Strategies

- Argumentation

The ability to use one's skills in a given context is called *application*. In other words, using the skills one has acquired through education or training constitutes the application of one's skills and knowledge. For instance, someone who has majored in languages might be able to use his or her language skills to interpret at an international conference. Of course, prospective employers, colleges, and universities are naturally interested in what you know and how well you know it. However, they are especially interested in whether or not you can *apply* the knowledge and skills you have acquired to the job or research position for which you are applying.

We have provided a scenario that demonstrates the interconnected relationship among competencies, skills, and their applications. Use this exercise and the examples shown to record your own competencies, skills, and applications.

Exercise for Step II

COMPETENCY (that which you know; education/training)	SKILLS (the degree to which you can do something; ability)	APPLICATION (the context in which you use your skills; life/work experience)
• Advanced Gaelic Classes, Dublin University, Dublin, Eire, Ireland • Tutor, Beginning Gaelic, Boston College, Chestnut Hill, MA	• Fluent in oral and written Gaelic	• Member, The Gaelic League, New York, NY • Assistant coach, County Galway, Irish GAILLIMH, Football Team, Galway, Ireland • Translated, from Gaelic to English, paper on "Short History of Gaelic League," 2001

Step III: Determine Levels of Proficiency

Using the skills you identified in Step II, describe the levels or degrees of proficiency you have achieved in using them. The following list will assist you in completing this exercise. On the lines provided, add other qualifiers that best describe your degree of proficiency in using your skills.

accurate (in)
adept (in, at)
advanced (knowledge of)
alert (in)
competent
concise
conversant (in)
detailed (knowledge of)
effective (in)
empathy
exceptional
exemplary
expert (in, at)
extraordinary
fluent (in)
functions (well)
gifted
good (at)
great
high (degree of)
intermediate
    (knowledge of)
judicious
keen (sense of,
    understanding of)
knowledge (of)

master (master of)
perception (of)
perceptive
practical (experience in)
proficient (in)
relentless (in pursuit of)
rudimentary
sensitive (to)
skilled (at, in)
sophisticated
    (understanding of)
strong (sense of,
    background in)
successful (in, at)
uncommon
understanding (of)
unusual

_____

_____

_____

_____

_____

Step IV: List Your Credentials; Articulate Your Skills

In this step, you need to provide information regarding the degrees, licenses, and certificates that you have earned. You should also consider the experiences that were an integral part of acquiring those credentials. In addition, determine which of your skills are a result of your education and training.

Exercise A for Step IV

Professional Degree (business, law, medicine)

Credentials: _____

_____

Postgraduate (certificate)

Specialization: _____

_____

Credentials: _____

_____

Graduate Degree (doctorate)

Specialization: _____

_____

Credentials: _____

_____

Graduate Degree (master's)

Majors: _____

_____

Minors: _____

_____

Credentials: _____

_____

Undergraduate Degree (bachelor's)

Majors: _____

_____

Minors: _____

_____

Credentials: _____

_____

On the following worksheet, articulate the level or degree of proficiency you have achieved. An example has been provided.

Exercise B for Step IV

SKILLS	LEVEL/DEGREE OF PROFICIENCY (articulation of your skill)
Improvisation (music composition)	Gifted trombonist; expert in creating extemporaneous jazz idioms using folk elements indigenous to southeastern United States; master in use of counterpoint rhythms

Step V: Review Review the worksheets and exercises you have completed in Steps I through IV. Summarize this information by writing your five most important competencies and skills, along with the level or degree of proficiency you have achieved in using them. To determine which skills are most important, you must consider which of your skills best correspond to those needed to perform the job or the research position for which you are applying. Write these skills in draft form—for now. You will revise them as you complete the information requested in Chapter 3. The following factors might affect the skills and competencies you choose:

- Your career, professional, and/or research objectives

- The program or position for which you are preparing your CV

- The degree of importance you attribute to your competencies and skills as a part of the total presentation of yourself

As you review the data you have collected thus far, remember your objective, which will determine the data you include in your CV. For instance, our list of competencies might be similar to this example, which is written in the same format that you will use when you develop your CV.

Example: Relentless in pursuit of excellence in instruction; highly functional in environments that expect high degree of critical judgment, maturity, sympathy, and creativity in instructional methods; keen understanding and appreciation of diverse learning styles; proficient in evaluation of student performance on oral examinations

On the next page, you will find a worksheet to assist you in determining relevant skills.

Exercise for Step V

Competencies and Skills

1. _____
   _____
   _____
   _____
   _____
   _____
   _____

2. _____
   _____
   _____
   _____
   _____
   _____
   _____

3. _____
   _____
   _____
   _____
   _____
   _____
   _____

4. _____
   _____
   _____
   _____
   _____
   _____
   _____

Preparing Your Curriculum Vitae

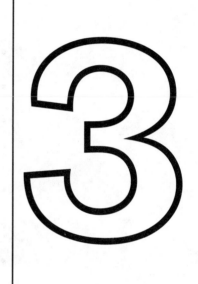

Now that you have established your competencies and skills, transfer them to a working draft of your curriculum vitae. This preliminary draft will reflect, in the broadest sense, the essence, structure, and components of your experiences as a graduate with credentials from institutions of higher education. Your CV will also include experiences that you have pursued after such study. Naturally, there are some common experiences that students and professionals in a wide range of occupations share and which should be reflected in a CV. After you prepare the working draft of your CV, read the remaining chapters of this book and carefully review the sample CVs in Chapters 5, 6, and 7. Then take a break, revise your working version, and prepare the final draft.

The following list comprises the major components, or defining characteristics, of a CV:

- Professional/Career/Vocational/Research Objectives

- Education

- Coursework

- Honors/Achievements/Awards/Kudos

- Thesis/Dissertation Abstract

- Research Interests

- Research and/or Laboratory Experience

- Teaching Interests and Experience

- Instrumentation Experience

- Specialized Skills

- Publications/Presentations/Works-in-Progress

- Work Experience

- Professional Associations/Learned/Scientific Societies

- Background

- Community Service

- Cocurricular Activities

- Interests

- Travel

- References/Letters of Recommendation

These components are not finite and therefore should be tailored to meet your needs. Adapt them to fit your experiences—use them, in fact, as a basis for creating components that more precisely fit your own situation.

The specific objective for which you are preparing your CV, as well as the order in which these broad components might appear on your CV, should reflect the degree of importance you attribute to them. Arrange them so that the most important information appears at the beginning of your CV and the least important at the end.

In the pages that follow, you will find descriptions of each component as well as suggestions to help you prepare your own preliminary, revised, and final versions of each component. Use the following four guidelines as you prepare the initial draft of your curriculum vitae.

1. Do not feel compelled to complete all the worksheets at one sitting. Begin with those that request routine information and then move on to those that might require reflection and detailed organization.

2. Initially, focus solely on content. Describe experiences in detail and later refine them through careful revision.

3. Ignore any overlap among components because some duplications or redundancies will be eliminated as you work through the drafts. Others can be edited or revised in consultation with your academic advisor, professor, or mentor.

4. Consider using one of the two options discussed below to organize the information in each component.

The first option is the self-teaching résumé, which can be used for curriculum vitae and provides templates for use with standard word-processing programs. Yana Parker has developed one such program that is a comprehensive approach to the preparation of templates. Parker describes the templates as detailed structural outlines of documents that provide a starting point and some graphic assistance in visualizing a finished product. These self-teaching templates also provide explicit instructions about the nature of the material to be entered in a particular section or location, along with instructions that link the various parts to form a focused, coherent, and concise document. She warns that your résumé will not look exactly like the templates and must be customized in the curriculum vitae format. In fact, she offers alternative wording for some components as well as optional components that are clearly appropriate for CVs.[1]

---

[1]Parker, Yana. *Resume Pro: The Professional's Guide.* Berkeley, CA: Ten Speed Press, 1993. Parker's "Self-Teaching Templates for your PC" (for IBM compatibles, in WordPerfect and Microsoft Word [including Windows]; for Apple Macintosh, in Microsoft Word) can be ordered from Yana Parker, Software Department #10, P.O. Box 3289, Berkeley, CA 94703.

The second option is to use any word-processing program to delineate the components, which allows for more flexibility and makes revising the document much easier throughout the whole process.

Professional/ Career/ Vocational/ Research Objectives

The first component of a CV states your objective(s), or the reason(s), you are distributing your CV. Your objective can be as brief as one sentence, stating a general goal, or as long as a brief paragraph, expressing both short-term and long-term goals.

Be sure to research carefully all graduate and professional programs and areas of employment that interest you. Connect your goals, which should be logically and clearly stated, to those of the program or position for which you are applying. Next, avoid vague or obscure language that fails to express precisely what you would like to do. Finally, use the worksheet that follows to prepare preliminary, revised, and final drafts of your objectives.

Professional/Career/Vocational/Research Objectives

Preliminary Version

_____
_____
_____
_____
_____
_____
_____
_____
_____

Revised Version

_____
_____
_____
_____
_____
_____
_____
_____
_____

Final Version

_____
_____
_____
_____
_____
_____
_____
_____
_____

Education   The objective of this component, as well as the component that describes your coursework, is to provide graduate and professional schools and prospective employers with a brief but thorough understanding of your academic background. In this section you should indicate the following:

- graduation dates

- degrees and the dates they were received

- diplomas

- certificates

- names of universities, colleges, professional schools, or other institutions you have attended

- your majors and minors along with your grade point average for each

- your cumulative grade point average for each institution attended as well as for each degree

Place all graduate degrees, as well as all completed coursework toward a graduate or professional degree, *before* your undergraduate degrees.

Highlight significant academic achievements, such as strong grade point averages in specific courses, as well as any extensive background you might have in areas of study outside your major and/or minor. If you are an undergraduate and a candidate for honors or high honors in your major, indicate as much in this component.

Education

Preliminary Version

_____

_____

_____

_____

_____

_____

_____

_____

Revised Version

_____

_____

_____

_____

_____

_____

_____

_____

Final Version

_____

_____

_____

_____

_____

_____

_____

_____

Coursework   Using your most recent transcripts, provide complete course titles, with brief descriptions where appropriate, so that prospective employers have a clear indication that course content is congruent with job requirements. You might also find it advantageous to list the grades you have received in some courses if you want to highlight academic performance or describe a trend in that performance. *Do not include course numbers or abbreviations because they are irrelevant and institution-specific.*

List all courses in groups that support and strengthen your professional, career, vocational, and/or research objectives. If, for example, as a German major and an accounting major, your professional objective is to pursue a position in financial consulting, we would suggest the following format for listing courses:

COURSEWORK

Accounting Courses
  Advanced Statistics
  Accounting Software Applications
  International Accounting
  Electronics Spreadsheet Analysis
  Business Management

German Courses
  Bibliography and Research Methods
  History of the German Language
  Heidelberger and Berliner
  Romantiker
  German Philosophers
  Seminar Clemens Brentano
  Seminar Walther von der Vogelweide

Coursework

Preliminary Version

_____
_____
_____
_____
_____
_____
_____
_____
_____

Revised Version

_____
_____
_____
_____
_____
_____
_____
_____
_____

Final Version

_____
_____
_____
_____
_____
_____
_____
_____
_____

Honors/
Achievements/
Awards/Kudos

List and briefly describe all special recognitions you have received, including study group participation, community and institutional service, departmental awards, athletic awards and/or lists, dean's awards, scholarships, fellowships, community awards, professional awards, academic awards, and memberships in academic organizations.

As a general rule, do not list high school awards or achievements since they might diminish the importance of undergraduate and graduate honors, achievements, awards, and kudos. If, however, you have significant high school awards or achievements you want to highlight, discuss with your academic advisor, professor, or mentor whether or not to include them.

Honors/Achievements/Awards/Kudos

Preliminary Version

_____
_____
_____
_____
_____
_____
_____
_____

Revised Version

_____
_____
_____
_____
_____
_____
_____
_____

Final Version

_____
_____
_____
_____
_____
_____
_____
_____

Thesis/Dissertation Abstract

Summarize your thesis or dissertation in a brief abstract. Include the full title and date or term of completion. Consult your academic advisor, professor, or mentor regarding the appropriate wording of this statement. Some disciplines (for example, chemistry and psychology) have specific editorial formats for abstracts. See Appendix C for appropriate stylebooks and manuals in your field.

Thesis/Dissertation Abstract

Preliminary Version

_____
_____
_____
_____
_____
_____
_____
_____

Revised Version

_____
_____
_____
_____
_____
_____
_____
_____

Final Version

_____
_____
_____
_____
_____
_____
_____
_____

Research Interests   Be as specific and precise as possible regarding the description of your research interests. Strike a balance between being specific enough to ensure congruence between your objectives and those of the program and/or employment option for which you are submitting your CV and being general enough not to preclude options that you might pursue if your research objectives are flexible. This delicate balancing act makes this component extremely complex and often requires that it be developed in consultation with your academic advisor, professor, mentor, representatives of graduate and professional schools, and/or a selected group of prospective employers.

Research Interests

Preliminary Version

_____

_____

_____

_____

_____

_____

_____

_____

_____

Revised Version

_____

_____

_____

_____

_____

_____

_____

_____

_____

Final Version

_____

_____

_____

_____

_____

_____

_____

_____

Research and/or Laboratory Experience

Provide detailed descriptions of your research and laboratory experiences. Include information about the ways in which your research fits into a given profession or into a particular laboratory's ongoing research. Be sure to give the title of each project as well as information concerning its actual or potential publication. Also, list the names and titles of professors or other individuals who have supervised or are currently supervising your research.

Research and/or Laboratory Experience

Preliminary Version

_____

_____

_____

_____

_____

_____

_____

_____

Revised Version

_____

_____

_____

_____

_____

_____

_____

_____

Final Version

_____

_____

_____

_____

_____

_____

_____

_____

Teaching Interests and Experience

For this component, describe only those teaching interests and experiences that can be documented. However, you might also include tutoring experience as well as any group learning experience in which you were a leader, such as laboratory or writing center experience.

Teaching Interests and Experience

Preliminary Version

_____
_____
_____
_____
_____
_____
_____
_____
_____

Revised Version

_____
_____
_____
_____
_____
_____
_____
_____
_____

Final Version

_____
_____
_____
_____
_____
_____
_____
_____

Instrumentation Experience   If you have used standard instruments in a laboratory—for example, computer hardware, photographic, or audio-visual equipment—describe that use. You will probably not need to provide extensive details regarding the devices themselves. On the other hand, if you have used state-of-the-art instruments, it is appropriate to describe both the instruments and the extent to which you have used them.

Instrumentation Experience

Preliminary Version

_____
_____
_____
_____
_____
_____
_____
_____
_____

Revised Version

_____
_____
_____
_____
_____
_____
_____
_____
_____
_____

Final Version

_____
_____
_____
_____
_____
_____
_____
_____
_____
_____

Specialized Skills
Use the information you developed at the end of Chapter 2 to decide which skills to include in this component. Describe in detail any interpersonal, leadership, organizational, or analytical skills you have as well as their applications and the contexts in which you have used them. Do the same for specialized skills involving any languages, computers/technology, computer software, and so on.

Students who intend to pursue a graduate degree should clearly describe their levels of proficiency in their intended field of study. Vague descriptions might be interpreted as a marginal degree of competency.

Specialized Skills

Preliminary Version

_____
_____
_____
_____
_____
_____
_____
_____
_____

Revised Version

_____
_____
_____
_____
_____
_____
_____
_____
_____

Final Version

_____
_____
_____
_____
_____
_____
_____
_____
_____

Publications/ Presentations/ Works-in-Progress

If you have authored or coauthored publications, provide appropriate bibliographic descriptions. List unpublished manuscripts only if they are actually being considered for publication. Artists and musicians, for example, should provide complete descriptions of works-in-progress. Provide detailed descriptions of presentations, particularly those made before academic societies and professional associations. Documentation should include title of the presentation, name of the organization, location of the meeting, and date.

Although classroom presentations would ordinarily not be included here, there are occasions when students are selected or encouraged to give a presentation because of superior performance in class or because they have researched a topic that is being studied in class. In these instances, such experiences should be listed. If you want to highlight significant classroom presentations, you might consider establishing a separate component for them.

Publications/Presentations/Works-in-Progress

Preliminary Version

_____
_____
_____
_____
_____
_____
_____
_____

Revised Version

_____
_____
_____
_____
_____
_____
_____
_____

Final Version

_____
_____
_____
_____
_____
_____
_____
_____

Work Experience

In this section, list all of your work experiences, including internships, summer jobs, and campus employment. Give brief but detailed descriptions of your responsibilities. Use action verbs to describe those responsibilities. (See Appendix A for a list of action verbs.) Provide the following information: titles, names of the organizations or businesses, locations of the organizations or businesses, and dates of employment.

For each individual entry, present information in the order of importance, as you deem appropriate. If, for instance, you want to emphasize your job titles, position them at the beginning of an entry. For example:

EXPERIENCE

Coach, Junior Tennis Teams, Hutto High School, Bainbridge, GA. Summer 1994

Recreation Assistant/Counselor, City of Bainbridge Parks and Recreation Program, Bainbridge, GA. Summer 1993

Research Assistant, Dean of Students Office, Bowdoin College. Wrote computer program for housing lottery. 1994

However, if you want to emphasize the organization or business where you have worked or volunteered, *that* information should be at the beginning of an entry. For example:

RESEARCH EXPERIENCE	FORD FOUNDATION, Lagos, Nigeria	1991
	Trained and monitored 300 rural women to enhance development potential of their indigenous association; formed Abo Umulolo Women's Cooperative as forum for installing motorised engines for cracking palm kernels and milling maze, beans, and cassava	
	UNICEF, Imo, Nigeria	
	Research Consultant 1990 Monitored and evaluated impact of participatory approach to Rural Drinking Water Supply and Sanitation Project	

Do not include the address or telephone number of an organization or business where you were employed; however, do include the city and the United States or Canadian postal abbreviation for the state or the province, respectively.

If your supervisor enjoys wide recognition in his or her profession, it would be appropriate to provide that information. Moreover, if you are seeking admission to a graduate program in a scientific area that requires clinical and/or work experience that was supervised by a certified professional, you *must* provide the name and certification of the supervisor. In addition, if an applicant seeking admission to a graduate program in clinical psychology has some clinical experience that was supervised, the clinical supervisor should be identified and that information should be included in the entry. Here is an example:

**CLINICAL
EXPERIENCE**

1993–1994 **UNIVERSITY OF MINNESOTA
MENTAL HEALTH CENTER**
Minneapolis, MN
Predoctoral Intern (APA approved)
Researched data on adjustment of first semester National Merit Scholars under supervision of Dr. Sven Lindstrom.

To ensure a comprehensive description of all of your experiences, discuss each item with your academic advisor, professor, mentor, or director of the career planning center at your college or university.

Work Experience

Preliminary Version

_____

_____

_____

_____

_____

_____

_____

_____

Revised Version

_____

_____

_____

_____

_____

_____

_____

_____

Final Version

_____

_____

_____

_____

_____

_____

_____

_____

Professional Associations/ Learned/ Scientific Societies

List any memberships in organizations such as in the American Chemical Society, the Modern Language Association, the American Psychological Association, the Mathematical Association of America, and so on. If you have not obtained membership in or an affiliation with a professional, learned, or scientific society of the discipline in which you plan to pursue graduate study or seek a position, you should do so as soon as you become eligible for membership. Such affiliation—or lack thereof—might be interpreted as an indication of the level of enthusiasm you have for your intended areas or fields of study.

One advantage of belonging to such organizations is that they publish scholarly journals and literature on major issues in their fields of interest. Frequently, they also convene national and international conferences that provide opportunities for interaction with other scholars. Furthermore, they are generally a rich source of information regarding opportunities for job placement within their fields.

You will find a selected list of major United States and Canadian professional, learned, and scientific societies in Appendix B.

Professional Associations/Learned/Scientific Societies

Preliminary Version

_____
_____
_____
_____
_____
_____
_____
_____

Revised Version

_____
_____
_____
_____
_____
_____
_____
_____

Final Version

_____
_____
_____
_____
_____
_____
_____
_____

Background

This component anticipates the section on graduate and professional school applications where applicants are asked to provide additional background or information that might not have been requested in other sections of an application. In addition, this component might include information regarding citizenship, prolonged residence abroad, and/or unusual educational or work experiences. For example:

BACKGROUND

Dual Japanese/Canadian citizenship with permanent residence in the United States. Past residence in the Netherlands and Canada. Fluent in Japanese; conversant in Dutch.

Background

Preliminary Version

_____

_____

_____

_____

_____

_____

_____

_____

Revised Version

_____

_____

_____

_____

_____

_____

_____

_____

_____

Final Version

_____

_____

_____

_____

_____

_____

_____

_____

Community Service   This component includes volunteer work, contributions to a community, and/or membership on university-wide committees. There might be some overlap for undergraduates between this component and cocurricular activities.

Community Service

Preliminary Version

_____
_____
_____
_____
_____
_____
_____
_____
_____

Revised Version

_____
_____
_____
_____
_____
_____
_____
_____
_____

Final Version

_____
_____
_____
_____
_____
_____
_____
_____

Cocurricular Activities   List and describe campus programs and activities in which you have been an *active* participant, such as student government, athletics, sororities, fraternities, academic clubs, and language clubs.

Cocurricular Activities

Preliminary Version

_____
_____
_____
_____
_____
_____
_____
_____

Revised Version

_____
_____
_____
_____
_____
_____
_____
_____

Final Version

_____
_____
_____
_____
_____
_____
_____
_____

Interests   This component includes avocations such as bird-watching, stamp collecting, chess, rugby, antique collecting, and music. List interests as a separate component even though they may appear elsewhere in your CV.

Interests

Preliminary Version

_____

_____

_____

_____

_____

_____

_____

Revised Version

_____

_____

_____

_____

_____

_____

_____

Final Version

_____

_____

_____

_____

_____

_____

_____

Travel Include extended international travel as a result of academic study abroad; however, do not include brief visits abroad as a tourist. If, on the other hand, you have had extensive domestic travel that is related to your objectives, mention it here. When appropriate, list cities, states, regions, or countries alphabetically with descriptions of experience and length of visits. For example:

ACADEMIC STUDY ABROAD

Sea Semester, Greece, summer of 2000
Semester spent on schooner to study marine life and to maintain ship

Travel

Preliminary Version

_____

_____

_____

_____

_____

_____

_____

Revised Version

_____

_____

_____

_____

_____

_____

_____

_____

Final Version

_____

_____

_____

_____

_____

_____

_____

_____

References/ Letters of Recommendation

This component is entirely optional; however, if you choose to include references on your CV, *list only the names and titles of individuals you have asked to write recommendations for you.* Including letters of recommendation depends on the preference of the employing institution or university to which you are applying. Some institutions maintain placement files and/or dossiers for students; therefore, requests for recommendations are generally referred to undergraduate institutions or to the institution of your most recent attendance. If appropriate, you may simply indicate one of the following on your CV:

1. Placement credentials available from the name of the institution or the name of the appropriate office

2. References available upon request

Professors, deans, chairs, and those who supervise your work are frequently asked to be references. Be sure to ask these individuals in advance for their permission to use them as references.

References/Letters of Recommendation

Preliminary Version

_____

_____

_____

_____

_____

_____

_____

_____

Revised Version

_____

_____

_____

_____

_____

_____

_____

_____

Final Version

_____

_____

_____

_____

_____

_____

_____

_____

Polishing Your Work

Thus far, attention has been focused on the content of your CV without regard to such matters as audience, writing conventions, and document design (format, layout, and so on). To be effective, your CV must be not only informative but also aesthetically pleasing, grammatically correct, and stylistically sound. This chapter provides some guidelines that will assist you in making decisions regarding the physical rendering of your CV.

Audience

The curriculum vitae is used to communicate with colleagues who share a common vocabulary and knowledge of a particular discipline. It is essential that you describe your experiences in language appropriate to your discipline. *Also, this is not the time to be modest—be your own advocate!*

Writing Conventions, Grammar, and Style

Use a confident, authoritative, and crisp writing style, as well as standard writing conventions throughout your CV. (See Appendix C for a selected bibliography of stylebooks and manuals.) Be concise, economical, and consistent in content and format. Use telegraphic style and avoid the use of first-person singular pronouns. Use definite articles selectively.

Grammar and spelling must be perfect, so follow standard grammar and punctuation rules. Use active voice and tenses that are always in agreement with the time of the action, as well as parallel structures and grammatical phrases. Avoid using exclamation points and interjections.

Where appropriate, use standard postal abbreviations and be consistent in this usage throughout your CV—for example, NM for New Mexico, AK for Arkansas, ON for Ontario, and QC for Quebec.

Ask several colleagues to critique a draft of your CV, and request a similar critique from your academic advisor, professor, or mentor. Recognize that you might not agree with some or all of the critiques that this process will generate. It is essential that you are able to justify, to your own satisfaction, the content and format of your CV.

Since you are making a first impression on representatives from colleges, universities, and prospective employers, *your CV must be perfect.* We, therefore, highly recommend that you carefully revise, edit, and proofread each draft of your CV. We define *revising, editing,* and *proofreading* in the following ways:

- *Revising:* Making critical changes to content and organization

- *Editing:* Making appropriate changes to sentence structure, basic grammar, and word choice

- *Proofreading:* Correcting spacing errors, typographical errors, misspellings, and mechanics

Make a hard copy of the final draft of your CV and accompanying correspondence and keep everything on file. Update your CV every year or as frequently as you have new information to add.

Document Design

Use a computer to create your curriculum vitae. CVs printed on laser printers look the best, but those printed by DeskJet printers are acceptable. Choose both a font style (e.g., Times New Roman or Tahoma) and a size (10- or 12-point) that are conservative, attractive, and reader-friendly. Use single spacing within a component and double spacing between components. Indent to improve readability and use liberal white space.

For variety and emphasis, highlight various levels of information by using underlining, capitalization, boldface, and italics. If you use full capitalization, do not underline and do not repeat the same highlighting technique for more than one level of information. (See Chapters 5 and 6 for examples.)

Avoid lengthy descriptions of academic and work experiences. Descriptions of six lines or more are difficult to scan and, therefore, limit readers' ability to orient themselves on the page, so choose content wisely.

Correspondence for the Application Process and the Job Search

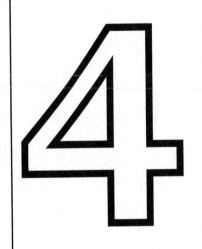

The same techniques used to polish your CV must be used to compose effective correspondence with individuals and organizations that might advance your career or vocational goals. Effective correspondence is an essential component in the application or job-search process. The correspondence that accompanies a curriculum vitae is generally referred to as a *cover letter*. It is defined, shaped, and determined by its diverse purposes. There are, for example, letters of application, declination, acceptance, and referral. In addition to the cover letter, the application process and the job search might require you to write other forms of correspondence such as prospecting letters, search firm letters, thank-you letters, letters of withdrawal, and letters of interest.

Objectives of Correspondence[1]

A well-written letter satisfies the following objectives:

- It offers the writer an opportunity to target the curriculum vitae to a particular person.

- It allows the writer to direct particular attention to specific skills that might be important to the reader.

- It enables the writer to state clearly why an organization is of interest to him or her.

- It opens the door for further communication and follow-through.

The essential structure and format of the correspondence should adhere to some commonly agreed upon guidelines even though there is wide flexibility regarding important matters of content, tone, style, and focus. While you are naturally expected to exercise prudent judgment in these matters, your primary consideration must always be to produce prose of the highest and most inspired quality.

Write with clarity, persuasion, honesty, and economy. You cannot afford to do otherwise. Grammar, writing conventions, style, format, and appearance require the same focused attention that you give your curriculum vitae. Use a computer and a laser or DeskJet printer, and proofread your correspondence several times to catch misspellings, typographical errors, grammatical errors, and ineffective style and format. This correspondence speaks for you at the most important stage of your application or job search—that initial stage when decisions are made that will determine whether you receive an interview or remain in a pool of applicants who do not survive the paring process.

Characteristics of Effective Correspondence[2]

- Address your letter to someone who has authority to hire you or to have an impact on your admission (or acceptance). Wherever possible, address a specific person, not a title.

---

[1]Adapted from *The Resume Handbook,* by Arthur D. Rosenberg and David V. Hirer, Holbrook, MA: Adams Media Corps, Inc., 1999.

[2]Adapted from *Resume Pro: The Professional's Guide,* by Yana Parker. Berkeley, CA: Ten Speed Press, 1993.

- Use that person's name and title, and spell both correctly.

- Find out as much as you can about the organization from which you are seeking employment (or admission).

- Sound enthusiastic to indicate interest.

- Be professional, warm, and friendly.

- Be specific about what you are seeking and what you are offering.

- Set yourself apart from other applicants. Identify at least one thing about you that is unique—something that distinguishes you and that is relevant to the position or program for which you are applying.

Guidelines for Effective Correspondence

Eric Martin and Karyn Longhorne, authors of *How to Write Successful Cover Letters*, provide valuable information and creative exercises that describe the process of self-assessment—a systematic evaluation of your strengths, interests, and personal style—that is a critical preliminary step before you prepare your correspondence. They also provide useful information that will help you determine what you need to know about the individuals and organizations to whom you direct your correspondence.[3]

- Effective communication involves shared understandings. Enhance the quality of your communication by using keywords and phrases about your skills as well as information from your profession or discipline, advertisements, descriptive pamphlets, brochures or films, and any other source that will show you have a clear understanding of yourself and have carefully researched the organizations or individuals with whom you are now communicating.

---

[3]Martin, Eric R., and Karyn E. Longhorne. *How to Write Successful Cover Letters*. Lincolnwood, IL: VGM Career Horizons, 1994.

- It is essential that the tone of the correspondence accurately reflect the tenor of the messages you want to convey. Be certain that your language and the format of your correspondence reflect such positive characteristics as career maturity, enthusiasm, intelligence, creativity, energy, organization, attention to detail, and skills appropriate to your focused interest.

- In some cultures, especially in academia, it is sometimes considered "bad form" to view or even use accompanying correspondence, CVs, and other accoutrements of the application or job-search process as marketing tools. While it is quite understandable that marketing oneself might clash with the values of some cultures, it is nonetheless naïve to assume that it is not part of competition for positions. Weigh your values against the advantages of using correspondence and CVs as effective marketing tools in your profession.

- Richard Beatty, author of *The Perfect Cover Letter*, insists that correspondence should generally be written so that it is directly related to the way it will likely be read.[4] Analyze your audiences' expectations and needs. This approach naturally shifts the focus away from writer-centered correspondence toward the needs of the individual or organization for which it is intended, requiring an astute ability to read between the lines. To take this approach, ask yourself which of your skills will most likely appeal to the reader and include them, thus, effectively targeting your audiences' expectations and needs. The between-the-lines information represents the nuances of effective correspondence that are rarely *stated* but which are often *inferred*. The classic example is the individual who applies for one position but who is offered another position because his or her unique talents surface during the course of effective correspondence. While this is not a common occurrence, it is, nonetheless, an eventuality that resourceful individuals create for themselves.

- Correspondence should generally be limited to one page. However, this is not an inflexible guideline. There are occasions when it is appropriate or even

---

[4]Beatty, Richard H. *The Perfect Cover Letter.* New York: John Wiley & Sons, 1997.

expected that correspondence will exceed one page. Correspondence regarding grant applications or communication with professional associations and learned societies exemplifies occasions when you must focus on the content of the communication rather than on some arbitrary rule regarding length.

- It is important to provide detailed information specific to the purpose of your correspondence, e.g., the date you will begin employment, your response to salary and benefits packages, or information regarding individuals who have agreed to write letters of recommendation.

- Appropriate and specific information describing your education and work background, skills, interests, publications, and presentations—in short, highlights from your CV that should generate enthusiasm in the reader for more detailed information about you—should be included.

- All correspondence should describe the actions you will take following the communication, i.e., thank-you letters and continuing interest letters.

The next section of this chapter provides several sample letters that will assist you in preparing effective correspondence. Please note that these letters have been arranged in the order of the application and job-search process. Following the sample letters is a section explaining how to distribute and market your CV.

Application Letter: Modified Block Style

14 Overland Street
Youngstown, OH 33602-1110
15 October 20__

His Excellency S. K. Ghusayni
Embassy of Lebanon
2560 28th Street, NW
Washington, DC 20008

Excellency:

I am applying for the position of Assistant Professor of English at the American University of Beirut. Since the position, which was advertised in the *Chronicle of Higher Education*, requires some teaching at Université Saint Joseph, I am sending a set of my credentials to you and to representatives of the respective institutions. This is a particularly exciting position as I would be able to use my knowledge of Arabic and French, which would enhance the effectiveness of my English language instruction.

As my enclosed curriculum vitae indicates, I received a Ph.D., *magna cum laude,* with a major in English and Linguistics, from Yale University in 1994. Prior to that, I obtained a B.A., *magna cum laude,* in French, and an M.A., *summa cum laude,* in French Literature from the Massachusetts Institute of Technology. Moreover, during my Fulbright Scholarship for the study of French literature at the Sorbonne, I read extensively the works of writers from Algeria, Tunis, Martinique, and other Francophone countries.

The paramount experience that has influenced my decision to apply for this position, however, was a three-year teaching position at Mohammed V University in Morocco. Not only did I teach English, but I also developed an innovative program in Arabic using computer-assisted pedagogy. It was recognized as a major breakthrough in Arabic language instruction.

During the week of 18 February, I plan to be in Washington, D.C., and would like to arrange an interview with you at your convenience. I will telephone you next week to arrange that meeting. Please feel free to call me at 216/555-8209 or fax me at 216/555-8210.

Thank you for your consideration. I remain

Yours truly,

Zoltan M. Zantovsky

Enclosures: Curriculum Vitae
Book Reviews
Disk Containing Arabic Language Course
Letters of Recommendation

Response to an Advertisement Letter: Modified Block Style

2 Fisherman's Cove
San Francisco, CA 94682
February 20, 20__

Dr. Alva Marie Demetriades
Senior Vice President
The Johnston Wells Group
720 Writer Square
1512 Larimer Street
Denver, CO 80202

Dear Dr. Demetriades:

I am applying for the position of Research Associate at The Johnston Wells Group. The description of the position, as advertised in *The San Francisco Chronicle,* is congruent with my educational and work background in health care public relations. Having written speeches and researched the mechanics of the health care system for senior executives of health management organizations, public and private hospitals, physicians' consulting groups, etc., I have acquired the high degree of expertise in analytical and communication skills that define the position with you. Furthermore, my facility with state-of-the-art computer-assisted research in biotechnology augment those skills.

I have enclosed a portfolio of my writing along with a recent copy of my curriculum vitae. As this is a confidential search, I would appreciate an opportunity to speak with you concerning individuals whom I might approach for references. You can appreciate, I am certain, the delicacy of interlocking relationships in the highly interconnected field of health care public relations.

May I take the opportunity to congratulate you on receiving the International Public Relations Award for research on marketing support of health care providers? It is a fine tribute to the quality of the service offered by The Johnston Wells Group. I shall contact you regarding my response to your advertisement in three weeks. Should you need to contact me before that time, please call my 24-hour answering service at 415/555-6874.

Thank you.

Sincerely,

Omo J. Kacendar

Enclosures (2)

Continuing Interest Letter: Modified Block Style

P.O. Box 1872
Santa Fe, NM 87492
7 June 20___

Mr. Joseph Jackson
Editor
The Plain Dealer
1801 Superior Avenue
Cleveland, OH 44114-2037

Dear Mr. Jackson:

I am writing to inform you of my continuing interest in the position of Associate Sports Editor of *The Plain Dealer*. Your forthright expressions of confidence in my journalistic skills and publication background convinced me that I would grow and mature as a sports editor in the demanding yet supportive culture at *The Plain Dealer*.

You will be pleased to know that eager and oftentimes perplexed sports fans in Santa Fe read with interest the continuing negotiations among the Cleveland Browns, the city of Cleveland, and the National Football League in the 90s. Needless to say, I was enormously impressed by *The Plain Dealer*'s in-depth coverage of all aspects of the momentous decisions that confront all of the players in this pivotal episode in professional football.

A very interesting thing happened to me on my return to Santa Fe. Purely by chance, I met Mr. Michael Doerfler, a retired gentleman who was a sports columnist for *The Plain Dealer*. Let me assure you that he had some great stories to tell about milestones in professional sports in Cleveland. He regaled me with accounts of personal encounters with individuals from all levels of that segment of society. I am eager to become a part of that hallowed tradition.

Thank you again for your generous hospitality during my recent visit.

Sincerely,

Strobe L. Watson

Networking with Friends Letter: Full Block Style

Theta Kappa Psi Fraternity
University of Connecticut
203 Broad Street
Storrs, CT 06269-1008
March 25, 20__

Jed Aaron Smith, Jr.
Executive Secretary
Theta Kappa Psi Fraternity
University of Utah
Boulevard of the Americans
Salt Lake City, UT 84202-7600

Dear Jed:

Greetings from the cold, windswept tundra of Storrs, Connecticut, and its only bright spot this weekend of weekends! With several hundred graduating seniors of TKP from twelve schools in the northeast due on our campus tomorrow, we should have a great career fair. It was great seeing you and all the brothers at our alumni officers' gathering at the University of Florida. I tell you, the warm weather makes me seriously think of transferring there.

Just wanted to get off a quick note to you to let you know that I am indeed interested in the new position of Executive Secretary for Alumni Affairs at our national headquarters at Indiana University. Although I would prefer an assignment at the University of Florida or the University of Texas, I could live with Indiana University, particularly when it would involve such extensive contact with all of our chapters throughout the United States. I would greatly appreciate a good word from you to the search committee on my behalf. In fact, I plan to call Jim at UCLA and Bob at UNLV and take them up on their offer to intercede on my behalf.

All of this feels just right! With TKP growing in all parts of the country, our alumni will be assuming increasingly important responsibilities in the overall management of each of our chapters. Take care and have a great time on the slopes. See you at the University of Colorado next month. Just do it!

Fraternally yours,

Jared Angier Solomon
Alumni Secretary

Enclosure: Curriculum Vitae

cc: James M. Braithwaite
    UCLA

    Robert S. Pendergast
    UNLV

Prospecting Letter: Full Block Style

January 29, 20__

Ms. Daphne Lizbet Middlemiss
Photographic Director
ARTnews
40 West 38th Street
New York, NY 10000-2222

Dear Ms. Middlemiss:

Cats! I love them! You love them! Your recent photographic features on *Egyptian Cats at Court* and *Siamese Cats in Thai Arts* were riveting and captivating works of artistic expression. For that reason and the obvious cachet that your publication enjoys in photography and art, I have decided to apply for a staff photographer position at ARTnews.

It is fitting that I have made this decision after being informed by *National Geographic Magazine* that my set of photographs of Bengal tigers, as well as a diary associated with each shooting, will appear in its Fall 2003 issue. That exposure and the recognition I am receiving for my exhibition of photographs of the flora and fauna along the Amazon River support my strong interest in a position with you. I have enclosed a copy of my curriculum vitae and a set of slides, which describe the diversity of my photographic techniques, the equipment, and the materials I use in producing them.

Should you plan to attend the Art in Urban Landscape Biennial in Baltimore on March 30, 2004, I would like to speak with you about my interest in joining the staff of ARTnews. I will contact you in two weeks to arrange a meeting. Since I travel frequently, I am always in touch with my E-mail address at: drunning bear@hotmail.com.

Thank you for the wonderful photographs of cats. Muffin, my beautiful, moody, sensitive, bright, black and white cat, is peering at me from her exalted position in the middle of my desk. Does she know what I am doing?

Take care!

Cordially,

David (Shenandoah) Runningbear
25-10 Orchard Park
Charlottesville, VA 22391

Referral Letter: Modified Block Style

July 20, 20___

Dr. Hillary Theakston
Department of Psycholinguistics
Bloomfield Hall
University of Pennsylvania
Philadelphia, PA 19104-6226

Dear Mr. Theakston:

Dr. Anton P. Cleggart, Matthew J. Owens Professor of Linguistics at the University of Delaware, suggested that I contact you regarding postdoctoral fellowships in psycholinguistics at the University of Pennsylvania. Since you have had a long and distinguished career in this field, he even suggested that I approach you regarding the prospect of obtaining a fellowship under your supervision.

I am very enthusiastic about the prospect of continuing my research on the psychological impact of autism on language acquisition in preverbal four-year-old children. Your paper at the recent annual meeting of the American Psychological Association further stimulated my interest in working with you.

I have enclosed a copy of my curriculum vitae along with a letter of introduction from Dr. Cleggart. Please contact me by E-mail so that we may arrange a time to talk about my proposal.

Thank you for your consideration.

Sincerely,

Dr. Siobhan Y. Kaufman
University of Delaware
Department of Psychology
Spruce Hall
Newark, DE 19617
E-mail: siobhan@psych.edu.

Enclosures: curriculum vitae
            letter of introduction

cc: Dr. Anton P. Cleggart

Search Firm Letter: Full Block Style

1472 Rockland Estate
Hanover, NH 03744
August 8, 20__

Dr. Danielle Linton-Panko
President
Panko, Linton, Jawarski, Paolone & Associates
Research Triangle Park
Building 16-62
Durham, NC 24720-0001

Dear Dr. Linton-Panko:

Your article, "An Analysis of Einstein's 1905 Specialty Relativity Paper and Its Implications for Pedagogy in Technical Writing," which appeared in the *Journal of Technical Writing and Communication* (volume 25, number 1, 1999), is extraordinary research whose outcomes will have far-reaching implications for pedagogy in technical writing and communication. It has, therefore, made imminent sense for me to become a client with your firm, as I now begin my search for a teaching position in technical writing. Its highly regarded profile in this field, coupled with your reputation for placement success, made the choice of your firm inevitable.

I have enclosed a copy of my curriculum vitae, which describes my educational and work background. After a decade of quality experience at IBM and Argonne National Laboratory in hardware and software documentation, on-line documentation, research in writing, and technical journalism, I am now seeking a teaching position at a major research university or laboratory in the Boston area.

In addition to articles in *The New York Times, The Washington Post, The Los Angeles Times,* and *The Chicago Tribune,* I am now a syndicated technical/scientific columnist with Gannet Newspapers and the Associated Press. My most recent publication is the second edition of my book, *Technical Documentation on the Internet.*

Dr. Danielle Linton-Panko
Page 2

I am eager to speak with you about procedures for becoming a client with your firm. Please fax the appropriate information to me at the address above, or contact me by E-mail at: mpp@aol.com.

Thank you for your consideration, and I shall look forward to hearing from you. Please keep my inquiry confidential.

Sincerely yours,

Marva Pallante-Pezzenti

Enclosure: Curriculum Vitae

Targeted Letter: Full Block Letter

Ishmael Benjamin Herera
Department of Mechanical Engineering
University of Mississippi
Cobalt Hall, Room W
University, MS 38323

December 12, 20___

Nissan of North America
1000 Lake Shore Drive, Suite 900
Detroit, MI 48200-3222

Attention: Environmental Compliance Officer

In the November/December 2000 issue of *Environmental Waste Management,* it was reported that "Nissan of North America leads major auto companies in the United States by making air conditioning systems free of ozone-depleting CFCs available in nearly two-thirds of the 2001 models it manufactures." As a doctoral student in automotive/mechanical engineering at the University of Mississippi, I have followed closely the continuing efforts of automobile manufacturers to comply with environmental regulations of this type. Your firm's success has attracted the attention of researchers here at the University of Mississippi.

I am, therefore, writing to you to arrange a summer internship at Nissan of North America, which would provide me with access to data that details the results of your efforts in reducing ozone depletion.

If it is appropriate for me to work with you on this proposal or to contact someone else at Nissan, I would be pleased to do so. I will contact you next week regarding the next steps in the process of arranging this internship. Please contact me at the Department of Mechanical Engineering, University of Mississippi at ishmaelherera@olemiss.urns.edu.

Thank you.

Sincerely,

Ishmael Benjamin Herera

Thank-You Letter: Modified Block Style

May 5, 20__

The Honorable Svetlana Teraskova
Member of City Council
County Court House
The City of Lake Forest
Lake Forest, IL 60012

Dear Councilwoman Teraskova:

Please accept my appreciation for arranging my attendance at the extended meeting of the City Council of Lake Forest, Illinois, last month. As a result of that experience and my extensive conversations with you, I have decided to continue my graduate studies in urban affairs at the University of Chicago and will focus those studies on the gentrification of Chicago's northside neighborhoods.

Again, I want to thank you for expressing your enthusiasm for my studies and for the opportunity to discuss some of my ideas with you and your colleagues.

Sincerely,

Qian Xinzhong
16 Seventh Avenue
Topeka, KS 32130

cc: Mr. Abraham Troutmeyer
    Chair
    City Council
    The City of Lake Forest

Acceptance Letter: Full Block Style

February 1, 20__

Ms. Marianne Meadows
Commissioner
Kentucky State Board of Tourism
Capital Plaza Tower
500 Metro Place
Frankfort, KY 40601

Dear Ms. Meadows:

I am writing to inform you of my acceptance of your offer to become the director of the Kentucky State Board of Tourism effective June 4, 2003. Pursuant to the contract I have signed, I shall report for work at 10:00 A.M. on the above-mentioned date.

Please know that I remain enthusiastic about the development of tourism in the great state of Kentucky. The broad economic returns that can accrue to the residents of the state are certainly powerful incentives for vigorous and imaginative implementation of tourism programs.

I am eager to join my colleagues in this important endeavor. Thank you again.

Sincerely yours,

Davin P. McCormick
7 Kellogg Circle
Kalamazoo, MI 49032-3160

Enclosure: Contract

Withdrawal Letter: Modified Block Style

October 24, 20___

Mr. Nicholas Y. Spurgeon
Vice President for Human Resources
Toys "Я" Us, Inc.
461 Fromm Road
Paramus, NJ 07652

Dear Mr. Spurgeon:

I am writing to inform you that I am withdrawing my application for the position of Vice President for International Marketing with Toys "Я" Us, Inc. As you know, the sharp fluctuations in the securities markets have enhanced the value of the dollar, thus favorably affecting my current position. This has consequently reinforced my decision, which we discussed at length as one of the several options available to me, to remain in my current position. In short, that is what I will do.

Thank you for spending your very valuable time with me at each critical juncture of this decision. I am certain we will have occasions to share ideas regarding effective international marketing of toys as we vigorously pursue international markets for our products.

Enjoy your upcoming trip to Singapore.

Cordially,

Roberto Juan Castillo
9440 Lehigh Parkway
Fort Myers, FL 33711-6200

Declination Letter: Full Block Style

September 25, 20___

His Excellency Livingston Gomez Gotarz
Embassy of the Republic of Cote D'Ivoire
2424 Massachusetts Avenue, NW
Washington, DC 20008

Dear Dr. Gotarz:

Thank you for offering me the position of Assistant to the Cultural Attaché for Graduate Education at the Embassy of the Cote D'Ivoire. Unfortunately, I received your cablegram several weeks after I had accepted a similar position with another country and thus must decline your offer.

I am, however, encouraged by your continuing interest and support of the graduate studies of your students in the United States of America and expect that we will continue to have occasions to discuss our mutual interests in international education.

Thank you again for your kindness during my interviews and subsequent conversations with you. Please accept my standing invitation for tea when I am next in Washington, D.C.

With best regards,

Aiesha Sente-Mendoza
10-107 Magnolia Boulevard
Baton Rouge, LA 70666

Marketing and Distributing Your Curriculum Vitae

Effective marketing and distribution of your curriculum vitae and accompanying correspondence are as important as the quality of the material itself. Both require a comparable degree of creativity, thoroughness, and attention to detail in order to achieve the desired results. View the process of distribution, in and of itself, as an essential means of marketing yourself.

To be effective in your overall marketing effort, you need to use strategies that are consistent with your personality and do not exceed your comfort level about presenting yourself for evaluation. A reticent person should not use the same strategy as a gregarious individual who has strong interpersonal skills and who is interested in projecting that image. Marketing and distribution strategies should include:

- Congruence among your professional, career, or vocational goals and your marketing strategy. While diverse objectives require diverse strategies, at this stage, it is essential to be certain that the information on your CV complements your objectives.

- Research approaches and skills you have developed and honed through your academic experiences to obtain information about individuals and/or organizations you plan to contact. The quality of this research will naturally affect the approach and the information you include in your correspondence, the negotiation strategies you use in obtaining and conducting interviews, and the general outcomes of the complete process. *Know as much as you can about the intended recipients of your correspondence.*

- Self-management of marketing and distributing your correspondence, as well as all other aspects of your application process or job search. This means you must give careful attention to such matters as time management, record keeping, follow-up, and negotiation strategies. Know where you are in every step of the process and exercise control over each element to ensure desired outcomes.

Self-management can be one of the most nettlesome aspects of this emerging marketing and distribution strategy. Although some of the psychological issues involved in preparing a CV have been addressed in

Chapter 1, it is instructive, here, to address some issues regarding management style.

For some individuals, the worst time to seek a position is when they do not have one and must get one. The pressure to obtain a position can lead to the production of an inadequate CV and/or marketing strategies that reflect necessity rather than opportunity. Likewise, an impending application deadline can cause panic in some individuals and thus result in a less than outstanding effort.

Other individuals, however, are actually energized by impending unemployment or application deadlines and, in effect, do their best work under pressure. In some circles, it is a badge of honor to do things at the last minute. Whatever your management style, know its possibilities and its limitations. Structure and manage your marketing and distribution strategy accordingly.

Distribution and Marketing Checklist

This checklist will facilitate the effective distribution and marketing of your correspondence. Modify and adapt it to your needs.

_____ Consult your advisor, professor, or mentor regarding the distribution and marketing of CVs in your field.

_____ Cultivate the art of preparing lists, writing brief notes, and keeping logs of your marketing/distribution targets. Prepare lists of prospective recipients and rank them in order of importance to you. Also, keep track of all correspondence, as this information will assist you in maintaining effective follow-up.

_____ Keep the number of organizations and individuals you contact within manageable limits. While the distribution of a large number of CVs might engender feelings of accomplishment, the effective follow-up that is required might become impossible or at least difficult to manage. Consider mailing information at different times so that responses will follow at different intervals.

_____ Enclose a CV with applications to graduate and professional programs. Provide all the information that is requested on an application. Refer to your enclosed CV, however, when inadequate space is available for the information that is requested on the application or when you are instructed or encouraged to provide additional sheets for such information.

_____ Enclose a curriculum vitae and accompanying letter with applications for grants, fellowships, and scholarships, even though they may not be required. An attractive CV can enhance an application and should always be enclosed unless a fellowship, grant, or scholarship sponsor strictly forbids it.

_____ Submit a CV and letter when requesting information regarding a position that an organization has not advertised. Enclosing such a CV with a letter of inquiry precludes the necessity for follow-up correspondence to request it.

_____ Submit a CV and letter with employment applications or responses to advertised positions.

_____ Use only the best quality paper and matching envelopes for your CV. Consult your advisor, professor, or mentor regarding acceptable colors for CV paper in your field.

Sample Curricula Vitae

The experiences of the fictitious individuals described in the sample CVs that follow provide concrete examples of content, style, and format that will assist you as you present your own unique experiences. Listed here are the academic majors and professions for which we have provided sample CVs.

Undergraduate
African American Literature
Art
Chemistry
English
Geology
Neuroscience
Political Science

Graduate
Anthropology
Astronomy
Clinical Psychology
Computer Science
Economics
German
Mathematics
Women's Studies

Professional
Architecture
Business
Engineering
General Medicine
Law

We have also included our own CVs for the fields of Higher Education and Composition and Rhetoric. You will find these at the end of this chapter.

African American Literature

Curriculum Vitae

JUDE WESLEY GREEN

26 River Road	Box 928, Bowdoin College
Bainbridge, GA 31728	Brunswick, ME 04011
(912) 555-3973	(207) 555-0922

PROFESSIONAL OBJECTIVE

Ph.D. in African American Studies

RESEARCH OBJECTIVE

To develop psycholinguistic profiles through study of autobiographical narratives of ex-slaves of African descent in eighteenth-, nineteenth-, and twentieth-century America

EDUCATION

1996 B.A. Bowdoin College, Brunswick, ME

Major in African American Studies (GPA 3.7); minor in psychology (GPA 3.7) and computer science (GPA 3.6)
Cumulative GPA 3.7

Candidate for high honors in African American Studies

1994–1995 Tougaloo College, Tougaloo, MS
Studied linguistics, music, and anthropology

Summer 1995 Yale University, New Haven, CT
Studied psycholinguistics, African American literature of the Colonial Period, and computer applications for research in the humanities

COURSEWORK

African American Studies
African American History
The African Diaspora
Race and Ethnicity
African American Fiction
Africa and the Slave Trade
Computer Science
Microcomputing Concepts Applications
Advanced Microcomputer Topics
Microsoft Networking II
Visual Basic Web Programming

Psychology
Introduction to Psychology
Developmental Psychology
Personality
Language: A Developmental
    Perspective
Other
Swahili
Survey of American Literature
Printmaking
Forms of Narrative

JUDE WESLEY GREEN
Page 2

HONORS AND AWARDS

Phi Beta Kappa, Alpha of Maine. Bowdoin College, 1996

Dean's Award, seven of seven semesters, Bowdoin College

Abraxas Award for highest standing during first year, Bowdoin College

The George Duane Kimbrough Prize for Academic Excellence in Computer Science, Bowdoin College, 1995

The Adam Clayton Powell Scholarship for Excellence in African American Studies, Bowdoin College, 1995

SKILLS

Academic: Strong problem-solving, critical judgment, conceptualization, and research skills; effective in unstructured academic environments where initiative and creativity are encouraged

Languages: Conversant in Latin; proficient in reading Swahili and French

Computer: Word Processing: WordPerfect
Microsoft Word
Windows 2000

Spreadsheet: Excel

Programming: C, C++, Java (dBase III for AIX)

AFFILIATIONS

National Urban League
Association for the Study of African American Life and History

EXPERIENCE

Coach, Junior Tennis Teams, Hutto High School, Bainbridge, GA. Summer 1994

Recreation Assistant/Counselor, City of Bainbridge Parks and Recreation Program, Bainbridge, GA. Summer 1993

Research Assistant, Dean of Students Office, Bowdoin College. Wrote computer program for housing lottery 1994

Student Representative, Board of Proctors, Bowdoin College, 1993–1995

INTERESTS

Spirituals, philately, tennis, swimming

Art

PHOEBE A. PARKER_____
_____Box 207, Beloit College, WI 53511, (608) 555-2761 _____
77 Cypress Way, Palm Beach, FL 29073, (305) 555-1596_____

PROFESSIONAL OBJECTIVE
Independent artist supported by exhibitions and publications

A R T S H O W S	• Spring 1996 — One-person show of environmental sculptures and landscape paintings—series of seascapes emphasizing play of light on water with contrasting water pollutants in staged relief	**W O R K S • I N • P R O G R E S S**
	• Fall 1995 — Wright Museum of Art, Beloit College / Series of self-portraits dealing with test anxiety	Photographic images of blossoming (Independent Study)
	• Summer 1995 — Crispen Gallery, Palm Beach, FL / Series of oil paintings of children visiting a planetarium	
	• Spring 1995 — Notten Gallery of Art, Philadelphia, PA / One-person show of watercolors of artists at work	Portraits of growth stages of children through adolescence
	• Fall 1994 — The Gallery of the Department of Art and Art History, Beloit College	Series of photo-graphic images of players in Virginia Slims Tennis Tournament

- Dean's Award (GPA 3.3)
  Six of six semesters

- Senior Bench Chapter of
  Mortar Board, 1996

- Shirley Stewart Foster
  Scholarship for
  Excellence in Studio Art,
  1995

- American Pewter Guild
- Surface Design Association
- Wisconsin Women Sculptors
- Women's Caucus for Art

HONORS

AFFILIATIONS

Beloit College   Beloit, WI

B.A., May 1996

Major: Art and Art History (GPA 3.5)

Minor: Museum Studies (GPA 3.2)

Cumulative GPA 3.3

Candidate for honors in Studio Art

The Art Institute   Chicago, IL

Summer 1995. Studied sculpture

EDUCATION

Model	Model and Writer	Costume Designer
Department of Art and Art History (Studio Art), Beloit College 1995–1996	Blackstone Photographic Modeling Agency Minneapolis, MN 1995	University Theatre productions of *Barefoot in the Park, A Funny Thing Happened on the Way to the Forum,* and *Evita* 1995–1996

E X P E R I E N C E

Docent	Intern	Apprentice
Wright Museum of Art, Beloit College 1996	Museum of Modern Art New York, NY Catalogued acquisitions in Eskimo art collection Summer 1995	Pierre L. Lovin, environmental sculptor Madison, WI 1994–1995

Art and Art History

Basic Studio
Drawing I, II
Painting I, II
Sculpture I, II

Photography I, II
Ceramics
Art History Survey I
Senior Seminar in Art
and History

C O U R S E W O R K

Communication Arts

Stage Management
Scene Design
Costume Design
Arts Management

Related

British Literature I, II
Shakespeare
Psychology
Images of Modern Man
Astronomy

Chemistry

CLEMENTINE OPHELIA HARE

2 Quackenbush Lane
Tuscaloosa, AL 34586
(205) 555-5660
E-mail: cohare@hotmail.com

Newcomb College
Box TU 6071
New Orleans, LA 70118
(504) 555-2777

**PROFESSIONAL/CAREER/RESEARCH
OBJECTIVE**

A research position that requires background in organic synthesis and/or chemical identification through spectrographic techniques such as NMR, GC, IR, UV-Vis, and mass spectroscopy

EDUCATION

B.S., 1996, Newcomb College of Tulane University, New Orleans, LA; major in chemistry; GPA 3.3; cumulative GPA 3.2

1993–1994, University of Tennessee, Knoxville, TN

Summer 1992, University of Alabama, Tuscaloosa, AL; studied biochemistry and environmental geology

COURSEWORK

(*denotes courses taken at the University of Tennessee)

Introductory Chemistry I*, II*
Organic Chemistry I*, II*, III
Advanced Organic Chemistry
Physical Chemistry I, II
Advanced Inorganic Chemistry
Independent Research in Chemistry
Senior Research in Chemistry

Instrumental Methods
Calculus I*, II
Physics I, II
Biology I*, II*
Environmental Hazards
Natural Hazards
Environmental Geology and
    Natural Resources

Related courses: Intermediate Louisiana French
Cajun Art and Music of the Nineteenth Century
Roots of Western Civilization
The Modern Experience in the West
Mass Media, Mass Society, and the Individual

LABORATORY EXPERIENCE

Research Assistant, Chemistry Department, Newcomb College
    Under Dr. M. P. Norris, Spring 1996–Fall 1996
    Experimented with synthesis of B-amino ketones via enol boronates, as they pertain to natural products

Research Assistant, Chemistry Department, Newcomb College
    Under Dr. M. P. Norris, 1995–1996
    Experimented with SmI selective bond cleavage of carbon-oxygen single bonds

Research Assistant, Chemistry Department, University of Tennessee
    Under Dr. Craig Barnes, Summer 1994
    Synthesis of macro-cycle containing two transition metal atoms

Research Assistant, Chemistry Department, University of Tennessee
    Under Dr. Craig Barnes, Spring 1994, Fall 1994
    Synthesis of starting material for graduate student research

CLEMENTINE OPHELIA HARE
page 2

INSTRUMENTATION EXPERIENCE

- Nuclear Magnetic Resonance
- Infrared and Ramen Spectroscopy
- Ultraviolet and Visible Absorption Spectroscopy
- Mass Spectrometry
- Atomic Absorption Spectrometry
- High Performance Liquid Chromatography
- Gas Chromatography
- Fluorimetry
- Gel Electrophoresis

MEMBERSHIP

Younger Chemists, American Chemical Society 1996

HONORS AND ACHIEVEMENTS

Stella Florence Pettypiece Memorial Prize in chemistry for outstanding performance in first year chemistry 1992

Clarence Charles Zess Mathematics Prize for Excellence in Calculus II

Captain, National Championship Swim Team 1991

All-America, high school swimming 1990, 1991

Deborah Wingert Athletic Scholarship (swimming), University of Tennessee 1992–1994

COCURRICULAR ACTIVITIES

Varsity Swim Team, Tulane University 1994–1996

Varsity Swim Team, University of Tennessee 1993–1994

Big Brother/Big Sister, Newcomb College of Tulane University 1994–1996

Tutor, Chemistry Department, Newcomb College of Tulane University, Fall 1995; assisted students in Advanced Organic Chemistry

OTHER EXPERIENCE

Assistant to the Manager, Welsch Electric Co., Tuscaloosa, AL

Coordinated warehouse inventory with showroom inventory, Summer 1996

Coach, Tuscaloosa Swim Club, Tuscaloosa, AL, Summer 1995

Coach, United Swimming Clinics, Mercersburg, PA, Summers 1993, 1994

English

curriculum vitae

phillip hogarth hedgeworth

- box CDE, colgate station, hamilton, new york. telephone (315) 555-1234
- 4 stanton place, rochester, new york. telephone (716) 555-4569

---

literary interests

---

continued work in writing and poetry, focusing on the development of craft, image, and voice; study of psychological and cultural complexities of poems and poets; interest in works of pound, williams, lowell, bishop, plath, hayden, ginsberg, and rich

---

workshops

---

poetry writing workshop—professor bruce berlind

emphasized critique and discussion of form and content, experimented with syllable verse, sestinas, and various other rhyme and metrical schemes

short fiction workshop—visiting author david bradley

emphasized extensive revision of working short stories; four drafts written over course of three months. mr. bradley stressed combination of creativity and discipline

independent in reading and writing poetry—professor bruce berlind

month-long intensive study of modern poets such as richard wilbur, denise levertov, and ted hughes; also wrote and revised two or three poems per week and met with professor berlind for discussions

---

cocurricular activities

---

cofounder, colgate university poetry society, 1995
organized and participated in poetry workshops every other week. edited and published poetry in *the colgate maroon*

cofounder and assistant president, colgate literary society, 1995–1996
organized bureaucracy to tie literary aspects of the colgate campus together; ran poetry and short fiction workshops; organized faculty lectures and co-sponsored visiting writers; administered the first in a series of poetry, short fiction and essay contests; hosted informal group discussions on literary topics

poetry editor, the colgate maroon, spring, 1996. one of two colgate weekly newspapers

editor, the pallette and the pen, colgate's literary and art magazine, fall 1995
contributed poetry spring 1995, fall 1995, and spring 1996

member, amnesty international, colgate chapter, 1994–1996

member, students for environmental awareness, 1995

---

education

---

b.a., may 1996, colgate university, hamilton, new york
major: english, gpa 3.7
workshop, gpa 3.7
minor: history, gpa 3.4
cumulative gpa 3.4

phillip hogarth hedgeworth
page 2

---

coursework

---

english

workshops
poetry—professor berlind
*poetry—professor
   balakian
short fiction
independent reading and
   writing poetry
other
british literature I
british literature II
american literature
the novel I
the american novel
shakespeare
literature of the 17th
   century
*the brontes

history
growth of nation-states
   in europe
europe in crisis since
   1815
u.s. in vietnam (1945–75)
formation of the russian
   empire
history of american
   diplomacy
*seminar: problems in
   american diplomacy
cultural identity of
   europe

related
roots of western
   civilization
the modern experience
north american indians
international ethics
*ethics
*mass media, society,
   and the individual
introduction to religion
the buddhist tradition
comparative cultures
contract tradition in
   modern thought

*denotes spring 1996 courses

---

honors

---

dean's award for academic excellence; six of six semesters

edward wood scholarship 1995, academic excellence

allen poetry award 1996, literary excellence

runner-up, colgate winter poetry contest 1993

honorable mention, colgate literary society, fall 1995 poetry contest

honorable mention, world of poetry national poetry contest, summer 1994

selected member, colgate geneva study group, fall 1994; traveled throughout western europe; studied various
   international organizations in depth

---

other experiences

---

lifeguard, athletic department, colgate university, 1993–1995

student worker, case library, colgate university, 1994–1996

carpenter's assistant, alternative timber structures, summers 1993–1995
                richard g. smith, contractor, summer 1995
                robert g. rose, contractor, january 1993

lifeguard, marriot hotel, henrietta, new york, summer 1994

Geology

MARIA VALESQUEZ COLÓN_____

(permanent)	(until 20 June 2003)
2733 Willow Park Drive	University of Rhode Island, Box 8028
Golden, CO 80401	Kingston, RI 02881
(303) 555-9822	(401) 555-0630

EDUCATION B.A., June 1996, University of Rhode Island, Kingston, RI.
Major in geology (GPA 3.4) with primary interest in oceanography.
Cumulative GPA 3.3.

COURSEWORK

Geology

Physical Geology
Oceanography
Mineralogy
Petrology
Coastal Geology
Structural Geology
Marine Geology
Stratigraphy and Sedimentation
Invertebrate Paleontology
Applied Field Geology

Related Sciences

Chemical Principles I
Chemical Principles II
Calculus I
Computer Science II
Physics I
Physics II

Other

Economic Principles
Introduction to Philosophy
Psychology
Intermediate Portuguese
Political Science
History of Egypt
American Education
Mass Media

HONORS Dean's Award, six of six semesters
Phi Eta Sigma, honor society for first-year students, 1993
Recipient, The Camille and Henry Dreyfus Foundation Scholarship for National Merit Finalist studying chemistry or related sciences

SPECIAL SKILLS

Language:	Fluent in Spanish; conversant in French and Portuguese
Computer:	Languages: C, C++, DB2, IMS, Visual Basics, Java, COBOL

Maria Valesquez Colón
page 2

LABORATORY EXPERIENCE

Researcher: The Sediment History of the Pettaquamscutt River and Its Relation to the Narragansett Bay, RI. Dr. J. King, advisor. Fall 1994

Research Assistant, Lake Ontario Coastal Survey, Colgate University, Department of Geology. Dr. C. McClennen and Dr. P. Pinet, advisors. Fall 1995

Research Fellow, University of Rhode Island, Graduate School of Oceanography, Narragansett, RI. The Sediment History of Heavy Metal Pollution in the Pettaquamscutt River, RI. Dr. J. King, advisor. Summer 1994

Research Assistant, United States Geological Survey, Branch of Atlantic Marine Geology, Woods Hole, MA. Lake Michigan Lake Level Study: performed grain size analysis on cores. Dr. S. Coleman, advisor. January 1995

Researcher, Coastal Geomorphology, cuspidal beach formations and their relation to rip currents. Dr. C. McClennen, advisor. Spring 1995

Teaching Assistant, Mineralogy, University of Rhode Island, Department of Geology. Dr. J. Novacek, instructor. Fall 1994

INSTRUMENT EXPERIENCE

- Coulter Counter/Elzone
- Freeze Drier
- X.R.F.
- Rock Saw

- S.E.M.
- I.C.P.
- Piston Corer
- Shatter Box

- X.R.D.
- Freeze Corer
- Smith-McIntyre Grab
- Cryogenic Magnetometer

OTHER EXPERIENCE

Tour Guide, Enviro Tours, Everglades, FL. Conducted environmental tours of Central America. Summer 1995.

COCURRICULAR

- *Certified,* NAUI Openwater I SCUBA diver
- Position #1, Women's Cross-Country Ski Team, 1993–present; Captain, 1992
- Latin American Student Association, 1993–present
- Pi Beta Phi Fraternity for Women, 1993–present
- Cycling Team, 1995
- Geology Club, 1993–present

TRAVEL

Extensively throughout Spain, Portugal, Finland, Sweden, Denmark, and Norway; resided in Oslo, Norway for two years (1991–1993)

Neuroscience

SARAH RUTH EISENBAUM[1]

P.O. Box 92, Brandeis Station
Waltham, MA 02254
617-555-8677

7 Evergreen Court
Highland Park, IL 60031
708-555-9081

RESEARCH OBJECTIVES

Short Range:

Neural plasticity in the mammalian CNS, i.e., the capacity of brain cells to change as a function of experience or environmental demand; field properties of the retina during synaptic drug application.

Long Range: M.D., Ph.D.

EDUCATION

B.A., *cum laude*, June 1996. Brandeis University, Waltham, MA
Major in neuroscience (GPA 3.5); minor in Judaic Studies
Cumulative GPA 3.6
High honors in neuroscience

Summer 1995, Columbia University, New York, NY
Studied psychological measurement and applications of experimental psychology

Spring 1993, Swarthmore College, Swarthmore, PA
Studied Hebrew (intermediate level), modern Hebrew literature, comparative psychology, and genetics

COURSEWORK

Neuroscience

Introduction to Neuroscience
Inorganic Chemistry I, II
Organic Chemistry I, II
Genetics Physiological
Cellular Biology
Functional Neuroanatomy
Clinical Neuroanatomy
Fundamentals of Neurochemistry/Neuropharmacology
Fundamentals of Neurophysiology
Neural Cell Culture
Senior Thesis I, II

Psychology

Experimental Psychology
Quantitative Methods
Comparative Psychology
Psychology
Personality

Judaic Studies

Religion and Literature of the Old
 Testament: Through the
 Babylonian Exile
Classical Judaism

Intermediate Hebrew
Modern Hebrew Literature
Texts and Images of the
 Holocaust

------

[1]Information contained in the categories RESEARCH EXPERIENCE and SPECIFIC SKILLS is from the curriculum vitae of Dean Michael Cestari 1992, Colgate University, neuroscience major. The information in the category INSTRUMENTATION EXPERIENCE is from the curriculum vitae of Lisa Petronella 1992, Colgate University, neuroscience major. This information is used with their permission.

SARAH RUTH EISENBAUM
page 2

COURSEWORK (continued)

Other

Calculus III
Physics I, II
The American Novel
British Literature

RESEARCH EXPERIENCE

Senior Thesis. "The Afferent Gastric Vagal Fibers Are Critical in Food Related Drinking in Rats" Program in Neuroscience, Department of Psychology, Brandeis University. Thesis Advisor, E. L. Baum, Ph.D. 1995–1996
Examined the effect of selective vagotomy of both the anterior and posterior gastric trunks, selective vagal afferent denervation with capsaicin, and selective vagal efferent blockade with atropine on drinking caused by eating in rats

Research Assistant. Bonney Center for the Neurobiology of Learning and Memory, University of California, Irvine. Summer 1994
Supervisor, Dr. James L. Lee. Received NSF Grant
Examined role of specific nuclei of the amygdaloid complex involved in the amnestic effects produced by benzodiazepines in rats; observed role of nucleus of the solitary tract as a possible relay station between the peripheral nervous system in aversive memory formation in rats

Research Assistant. Department of Anatomy and Cellular Biology, University of Illinois, Champaign-Urbana. Summer 1993
Supervisor, Dr. Lois M. Rogers
Examined nerve growth factors receptors of chick and quail embryos using in situ hybridization and autoradiographic techniques

SPECIFIC SKILLS

Surgery (rat)

-Stereotaxic cannulae and electrode implantation
-Lesioning, electrolytic as well as chemical via microinjections with Hamilton syringe
-Full anterior and posterior trunk vagotomies including selective vagal denervation using capsaicin
-Gastric fistula implantation

SARAH RUTH EISENBAUM
page 3

SPECIFIC SKILLS (continued)

Histology

-Perfusion with saline and formalin
-Tissue sectioning using freezing microtome and Cryostat
-Microscope slide subbing and mounting of tissue on slides
-Lesion verification using projector and microscope

Staining

-Cell body (Cresyl violet)
-Direct immunofluorescence
-Indirect immunoperoxidase
-Autoradiography

Behavioral Training Testing

-Radial arm maze
-Inhibitory Avoidance (IA)
-Continual multiple-trial TA
-Water maze
-Y-maze

Cell Culture

-Aseptic technique
-Preparation of primary cultures of Schwann cells from rat sciatic nerve
-Preparation of mixed cultures of oligodendrocytes and astrocytes from neonatal rat brain
-Staining techniques mentioned above

INSTRUMENTATION EXPERIENCE

(1) Cell Culture
-sterile and aseptic technique
-media preparation
-maintenance and preparation of primary cultures: Schwann cells, Astrocytes
-cell lines; PC12, B49, BSO
-transfected Schwann cells-SV40

(2) Molecular Biology
-plaque lifting screening
-immunological screening of a cDNA library
-isolation of mRNA
-Northern Blotting
-manipulation of plasmid vectors using restriction enzymes
-preparation and assay of bacteriophase lysates
-determination of concentration of cultures by antibody titer
-plasmid DNA purification

SARAH RUTH EISENBAUM
page 4

INSTRUMENTATION EXPERIENCE (continued)

(3) Biochemistry
-Western Blotting
-SDS-PAGE electrophoresis
-Silver Straining
-electro-elution
-scanning densitometry
-Lowry Protein Assay
-cell fractionation
-Differential Centrifugation
-gradient gels
-UltravioletNisual Spectroscopy
-Enzyme Linked Immunosorbent Assay

(4) Biology
-Transmission Electron Microscopy
-Scanning Electron Microscopy
-Nissl Staining
-Audioradiography

COMMUNITY SERVICE

Volunteer, Department of Psychological Services, Brigham and Women's Hospital, Boston, MA
Supervisor: Dr. Dawne Allette-Noel, specialist in study of Alzheimer's disease. 1994

Volunteer, Neurobiology Division, The Massachusetts Mental Health Center, Boston, MA
Supervisor: Dr. Sander Gorham. 1995
Counseled patients in early stages of Parkinson's disease.

Circulation Assistant, Gerstenzang Science Library, Brandeis University. 1993–1994

Political Science

Curriculum Vitae

YOKO I. NAKAGAWA

Box 903 College Station • Norman, OK 73069 • (405) 555-2187

6 Jackson Way • Seattle, WA 98100 • (206) 555-4563

BACKGROUND

Dual Japanese/Canadian citizenship with permanent residence in the United States. Past residence in the Netherlands and Canada. Fluent in Japanese; conversant in Dutch.

EDUCATION

B.S., June 1996. University of Oklahoma, Norman, OK. Major in political science; minor in geography. Cumulative GPA 3.5. Candidate for high honors in political science.

RESEARCH INTERESTS

The nature of concept formation and theory construction in political science with particular emphasis on utopian impulses in political philosophy.

COURSEWORK

Political Science

Introductory I
Comparative European Politics
American Political System
National Institutions and the Policy Process
Parties in the Political Process
European Security and Integration
National Security
Family in Political Thought
Living Politicians: The Electoral Process

Geography

Human Geography
Political Geography
Geography of Development: Asia
Environmental Geography
Environmental Issues
Environmental Hazards
Environmental Impact Assessment

Related

Calculus I
Elementary Russian I, II
Oceanography
Introductory Economics
Living Writers
Modern Philosophy

Aquatic Insects
Chinese Studies
World Food and Hunger
Comparative Cultures
Social and Political Ethics

YOKO I. NAKAGAWA

HONORS

Pi Sigma Alpha, national political science honorary society.

Dean's Award (3.3 GPA). Five of six semesters.

Member, American University London Study Group. Studied political and economic policies of the European community. Achieved 3.7 GPA. Spring 1993.

Colonel J. G. McCoy Scholarship. Research paper, "China: A Ten-Year Prediction." Received $3,000. 1993. *Research Assistant* to Mary Margaret McShane, Ph.D., Distinguished Professor of Political Institutions, The Carl Albert Congressional Research and Study Center, the University of Oklahoma. Analyzed document of funding sources of independent political parties for Dr. McShane's book, *Political Action in the Eighties: Americans Outside of the Political Mainstream.* 1996.

EXPERIENCE

Kappa Kappa Kappa Sorority. 1993–present.

> *Steward.* Administered budget of $52,000. Directed preparation of all meals; organized modernization of kitchen facilities; supervised five student workers and cook. Fall 1994.

> *Social Manager.* Administered budget of $16,000. Spring 1995.

> *Scholarship Chair.* Organized tutoring program; originated sorority computer center. Fall 1995.

> *Member.* Sorority Executive Committee. 1995–present.

Intern, Daiwa Securities Co., London, England.
Assisted head trader of United Kingdom Equities Division in product research; observed trading procedures of London Stock Exchange. Spring 1993.

Intern, Nikko Securities Co., New York, NY.
Aided in assembling daily trade information for brokers; planned study program of the New York Stock Exchange for Nikko interns. Summer 1994.

Intern, United States Senator Alphonse D'Amato (R-NY), Washington, DC.
Aided legislative assistant in researching legislation and reporting on committee hearings. Gained familiarity with structure of Capitol Hill and Senate offices. January 1995.

Volunteer, Saracens Rugby Club, London, England.
Assisted in coaching and managing rugby team for girls ages ten through twelve. Spring 1993.

COCURRICULAR

Representative. Student Affairs Board. 1993–1994.

President's Committee on Investments. 1995.

Asian Society. 1994–present.

SKILLS

Conversant with political issues at all levels of government; practical experience in problem solving; excellent oral and written communication skills.

Anthropology

NGOZI AWOJOBI   **Curriculum Vitae**

BACKGROUND Nigerian citizen with permanent residency in the United States of America; extended residency in England, Canada, and Barbados; fluent in Igbo, Swahili, Yoruba, English, and French; advanced knowledge of computer systems and applications in social science research.

PRESIDENT	THE NGAMI MFUMBIRO FOUNDATION	2000–present
	Lagos, Nigeria, and Washington, DC	

Manage a by-invitation coterie of African, Middle Eastern, and Near Eastern countries, which support economic, educational, and scientific development in their respective countries; supervise staff of 75 consultants in Lagos office and 200 in Washington; manage annual budget of $50 million; report to Board of Advisors composed of representatives of participating countries and funding areas.

October–February
2107 R Street, NW
Washington, DC 20009
202/555-3187 (tel)
202/555-3189 (fax)

March–September
PMB 1209, Sijuada
Lagos, Nigeria
(1) 6120789 (tel)
28763 (telex)
(1) 6120663 (fax)

nawojobi@hotmail.com
http://www.nawojobi.org

ACCOMPLISHMENTS

- Increased endowment from $120 million

- Increased awards, grants, scholarships, fellowships by fifty percent in four years

- Expanded scope of scientific grants to include telecommunications and aerospace engineering

- Developed innovative program for recruiting expatriate scholars for positions at universities and research institutions in their home countries

- Actively established cooperative projects with other international foundations with similar interests

- Organized and managed development staff that continually seeks innovative sources of funding for foundation projects

NGOZI AWOJOBI

SUMMARY OF QUALIFICATIONS

- Dedicated to efforts to improve the quality of life of all people, especially those in Africa, the Near East, and the Middle East
- Successful in bringing diverse opinions and ideas to consensus
- Innovative thinker and problem solver
- Excellent communication and persuasion skills
- Effective in conceiving, developing, and implementing creative programs targeted for special populations

EDUCATION

HARVARD UNIVERSITY, Cambridge, MA

Ph.D., anthropology, *summa cum laude*   1985

Major: cultural anthropology

Dissertation, awarded High Honors: "The development of anthropological writing as it has moved through culture critique: the use of knowledge of other cultures to examine the assumptions of our own"

Areas of specialization:
- Socioeconomic transformation of indigenous societies and their transition to market economies
- Transformation of indigenous local organizations into development organizations

Research interests:
- Symbolic analyses of women and rituals in Igbo culture
- Ethnic formation and transformation—the Arolgbo ethno-history

AHMADU BELO UNIVERSITY, Zaria, Nigeria

M.A., cultural anthropology, African History (Honors)   1982

Thesis: "Comparative analyses of kinship, marriage, and family in matrilocal societies in Nigeria"

UNIVERSITY OF IBADAN, Ibadan, Nigeria

B.A., geography and mathematics, Honors   1978

HONORS
and AWARDS

Senior Fulbright Scholar-in-Residence, SUNY, Farmingdale, NY

International Fellow, American Association of University Women Award for dissertation

Research Fellow, Rockefeller Foundation, Ahmadu Bello University

Faculty Prize for Best Graduating Student, Ahmadu Bello University

NGOZI AWOJOBI   **page three**

RESEARCH   FORD FOUNDATION, Lagos, Nigeria   1991
EXPERIENCE   Trained and monitored 300 rural women to enhance development potential of
                   their indigenous association; formed Abo Umulolo Women's Cooperative as
                   forum for installing motorised engines for cracking palm kernels and milling
                   maze, beans, and cassava

               UNICEF, Imo, Nigeria
                   Research Consultant   1990
                   Monitored and evaluated impact of participatory approach to Rural Drinking
                   Water Supply and Sanitation Project

               ROCKEFELLER FOUNDATION, Lagos, Nigeria   1990
                   Used anthropological and historical theories and methods, especially oral
                   traditions, in study of the Aro of southeastern Nigeria

TEACHING   HARVARD UNIVERSITY, Cambridge, MA. Teaching Fellow   1992
EXPERIENCE   Courses taught:
                       -Film and Anthropology: The Translation of Culture
                       -Economic Anthropology

               BOSTON COLLEGE, Chestnut Hill, MA. Assistant Professor   1991
                   Courses taught:
                       -Economic Anthropology
                       -Race and Society

               UNIVERSITY OF NIGERIA, Nsukka. Professor, Department Chair   1990
                   Courses taught:
                       -Anthropological Theories
                       -Marxist Sociology
                       -Rural Development Studies
                       -Systems of Social Inequality
                       -Women and Development

PUBLICATIONS   Awojobi, Ngozi. *The Aro of Southeastern Nigeria.* Ibodan, Nigeria: University of Nigeria Press, 1994.

               ———. *Economic Anthropology.* Washington: Smithsonian Institution Press, 1994.

               ———. "Women in African Society: The Place of Igbo Women in Igbo Culture." *Nigerian Journal of Economic and Social Studies* 50 (1990), pp. 38–72.

               Awojobi, Ngozi, and Catherine E. Shu. "Cultural Ecology of Agrarian Societies," *Contemporary Readings in Sociology.* Chicago: University of Chicago Press, 1992.

               Awojobi, Ngozi, and Joi Chin. "Ethnology of the Near East and North Africa," *Signs* 85 (1989), pp. 56–66.

AFFILIATIONS   Association of African Women for Research and Development (AAWARD)
and BOARDS   Association of American Anthropologists
               Nigerian Association of Sociologists and Anthropologists
               Nigerian Economic Society
               Nigerian Academy of Science
               Nigerian Institute of International Affairs
               Social Science Research Council
               Society for Applied Anthropology

Astronomy

Curriculum Vitae   **AARON J. LEVY**

residence: 3 Rosebud Terrace   office: 4800 Oak Grove Drive
            Pasadena, CA 91102   Pasadena, CA 91109
            (818) 555-9079   (818) 555-6583
            Fax: (818) 555-9090   Fax: (818) 555-9854
            E-mail: alevy@aol.com   E-mail: alevy@net.com

EDUCATION

Ph.D., UNIVERSITY OF WASHINGTON   Seattle, WA
                                                                                 1992

        Major: astronomy
        Research interests: radio astronomy; optics; x-ray observations, stellar evolution

B.A., *magna cum laude,* REED COLLEGE   Portland, OR
                                                                                   1985

        Major: astronomy
        Minor: classics

RESEARCH INTERESTS

Optics; radio astronomy; stellar astronomy; extragalactic supernovae; optical systems and design; CCD photometry of extragalactic supernovae.

EXPERIENCE

    JET PROPULSION LABORATORY

                                                                 Pasadena, CA
        California Institute of Technology   1995–present

        Associate Research Astronomer

        Research interests: adaptive optics; charge-coupled devices; infrared dector arrays; interplanetary optical communications; telecommunication systems; artificial intelligence

        Manage $500,000 budget; supervise four post-doctoral research fellows, two Ph.D. candidates, and eight undergraduate assistants.

AARON J. LEVY

EXPERIENCE
(continued)

UNIVERSITY OF CALIFORNIA, BERKELEY

Berkeley, CA
1993–1995

Adjunct Assistant Professor of Astronomy

Research and
instructional
interests:

circumsteller molecular envelopes of evolved stars;
luminous hot stars (type O and B, and the Wolf-Rayet
stars); x-ray extreme ultraviolet and far interests: ultraviolet
observations of evolved stars; joint projects with Laboratoire
d'Astronomie Spatiale in Marseilles, France.

UNIVERSITY OF FLORIDA

Gainesville, FL
1992–1993

Postdoctoral Research Associate

Research interests: radio astronomy; dynamical and solar system astronomy; stellar evolution.

UNIVERSITY OF WASHINGTON

Seattle, WA
1991–1992

Graduate Research Assistant
Co-investigative Assistant, Infrared Astronomical Satellite, 1991.

NATIONAL RADIO ASTRONOMY OBSERVATORY

Charlottesville, VA
1990

Summer Research Assistant

GEORGIA TECH RESEARCH INSTITUTE

Atlanta, GA
1989

Summer Research Assistant

Research interests: infrared/electro-optics; microelectronics; millimeter wave technology.

SPECIAL SKILLS

Computer: Scientific software and hardware development; system modeling; database management;
mathematical modeling; IBM large-scale systems; UNISYS and VAX computers.

AARON J. LEVY

PUBLICATIONS

Journal Articles
refereed

A.J. Levy, T.M. Avery, O.L. Braun, "Optical identifications of high luminosity infrared sources," *Astronomical Journal,* 201, 1411–1420 (1991).

A.J. Levy, S.M. Smith, R.A. Quakenbush, "The Hubble Space Telescope: ultraviolet and x-ray observations," *Astrophysical Journal,* 80, 1202–1218 (1993).

Books

A.J. Levy, *Paths to the Present: Origins of Elliptical Galaxies,* John Wiley & Sons, Inc. 225 pp (1992).

A.J. Levy, *Directory of Observatory and Satellite Facilities in the United States and Canada,* John Wiley & Sons, Inc. Vol. 1,11. 400 pp (1993).

Thesis

A.J. Levy, "Instrumentation in radio astronomy," Ph.D. dissertation, University of Washington, 275 pp (1992).

PRESENTATIONS

"Instrumentation in radio astronomy," oral paper, American Astronomical Society Meeting, Princeton, NJ, June 1991.

"An observational study of barium stars and their relation to Cepheids," American Astronomical meeting, Tucson, AZ, 1982.

"Infrared detector arrays," NOAA workshop on "Infrared Emission from Active Galactic Nuclei," Madison, WI, June 1993.

GRANTS

"Interplanetary optical communications," Arizona Space Grant Consortium, 1992.

Two-year grant of $50,000. Support for student and faculty wages, equipment, and travel to observatories to conduct astronomical observations.

GRANTS
(continued)

"Luminous Hot Stars," National Science Foundation, College Science Instrumentation Program, June 1993.

Two-year grant of $45,000, matched by University of California, Berkeley, for computer system to be used at University of California, Berkeley.

Travel grant of $5,000 from United States National Committee to the IAU to attend the International Astronomical Union General Assembly in Marseilles, France, 1995.

COMMUNITY SERVICE

Member, Ph.D. dissertation committees for T. L. Smith (Astronomy 1990–1992) and A.O. Schwartz (Astrophysics 1991–1993), University of Washington.

Member, Committee on Affiliation Services, Lick Observatory, University of California, Santa Cruz, CA.1990–present.

Member, University committee on user services, Kitt Peak National Observatory and Dominion Astrophysical Observatory. 1991–present.

PROFESSIONAL AFFILIATIONS

American Astronomical Society, 1987–present
Astronomical Society of California, 1990–present
International Astronomical Union, 1992–present
American Association of Variable Star Observers, 1987–present

Clinical Psychology

GISELA E. SCHMIDT

| home: 2764 Smythe Blvd. | Minneapolis, MN | (612) 555-4683 | Fax (612) 555-8710 |
| office: 1 Miller's Place | Minneapolis, MN | (612) 555-6723 | Fax (612) 555-2689 |

RESEARCH INTERESTS

Performance anxiety (academic and music); music therapy

EDUCATION

1994 **UNIVERSITY OF MICHIGAN**
Ann Arbor, MI
Ph.D., Clinical Psychology
Dissertation: "Assessing test anxiety, stress reduction, and self-concept maintenance among first semester National Merit Scholars"

1990 **UNIVERSITY OF MICHIGAN**
Ann Arbor, MI
M.A., Clinical Psychology
Thesis: "Psychophysiological investigation of the effects of positive personality reinforcements and degrees of uncertainty among Phi Beta Kappa inductees who are physics majors"

1987 **ST. OLAF COLLEGE**
Northfield, MN
B.A., *summa cum laude*, Psychology Minor: Music
Elected to membership in Sigma Xi and Psi Chi

HONORS and AWARDS

1993 Division 29 (Division of Psychotherapy)
Winner, graduate student competition for best paper on measurement, University of Michigan.

1987 Phi Beta Kappa, St. Olaf College

1987 Thomas J. Watson Fellowship for year of independent research in Bolivia, Turkey, Bulgaria, and France.
Topic: "The effects of lullabies on relaxation among autistic teens"

1986 Psi Chi, St. Olaf College

GISELA E. SCHMIDT

FELLOWSHIPS

1993 Dissertation Grant, Horace A. Rackham School of Graduate Studies, University of Michigan

1995 Postdoctoral Fellowship in Clinical Psychology, University of Rochester and Eastman School of Music, Rochester, NY

Focus: "Comparative studies of psychomotor dysfunction in breathing techniques among flautists and oboists"

LICENSES

1994 Licensed Psychologist, State of Minnesota
License #200

CLINICAL EXPERIENCE

1993–1994 **UNIVERSITY OF MINNESOTA MENTAL HEALTH CENTER**
Minneapolis, MN
Predoctoral Intern (APA approved)

Researched data on adjustment of first semester National Merit Scholars under supervision of Dr. Sven Lindstrom.

1990–1992 **UNIVERSITY OF MICHIGAN COUNSELING SERVICES**
Ann Arbor, MI
Half-time Psychology Intern

Supervised two master's level interns in counseling practica; taught counseling methods course and measurements course.

1989–1990 **UNIVERSITY OF MICHIGAN COUNSELING SERVICES**
Ann Arbor, MI
Half-time Psychology Intern

Conducted psychotherapy with graduate students pursuing degrees in music; performed psychological consultations and evaluations of anorexic clients under supervision of Dr. Hope Wilson Webber, Clinical Psychologist.

1989 **YPSILANTI PSYCHIATRIC CENTER**
Ypsilanti, MI
Half-time Psychology Intern

Performed psychodiagnostic assessments under supervision of Dr. Agnes Y. Kimbrough, Clinical Psychologist.

Jamal Marquis Magby   page two

_____

EDUCATION

■ Ph.D., 1993, Computing and Computational Mathematics, Stanford University, Stanford, CA

Dissertation: "On randomized versus deterministic computation"

Abstract: A study of the relative power of linear and polynomial randomized time compared with deterministic time.[1]

Related courses:
- Numerical Analysis of Dynamic Systems
- Advanced Numerical Analysis
- Advanced Methods in Matrix Computation
- Numerical Methods for Initial Boundary Problems
- Number Theory
- Artificial Intelligence
- Machine Learning
- Methods of Mathematical Physics

■ B.Sc., 1988, Computer Science and Mathematics, University of Hawaii, Honolulu, HI
GPA 3.9 (4.0)

Honors and Awards:
Alpha Theta Mu, honorary society in computer science
Omicron Delta Psi, honorary society in mathematics
Dean's Award (seven of eight semesters)
NCAA Scholar Athlete in Track (200 and 400 meters)

Related courses:

Mathematics
- Mathematical Logic I, II
- Representation and Memory
- Topology
- Real Analysis I, II
- Quantitative Reasoning
- Theory of Algorithms
- Geometry
- Differential Equations

Computer Science
- Theory of Computing
- Discrete Structures
- Operating Systems
- Simulation
- Information Systems
- Computer Graphics
- Compiler Design
- Artificial Intelligence

_____

[1]Karpinski, Marek and Rutger Verbeek. "On randomized versus deterministic computation." *Theoretical Computer Science,* 154, (1996), 23–39.

Jamal Marquis Magby   page three

PUBLICATIONS

Journal Articles

■ J. M. Magby. "New algorithms for signal processing and analysis" *Journal of Computer and System Sciences* 21 (1995) 423–475.

■ ———. "Notes on constructive logic and implications for computer science" *Mathematical Structures in Computer Science* 5 (1994) 162–183.

■ ———. "Numerical solutions of boundary value problems" *Mathematical Structures in Computer Science* 3 (1993) 122–145.

Book

■ Magby, Jamal Marquis. *Studies in Artificial Intelligence.* 3rd ed. New York: Academia Press, 1992.

RESEARCH EXPERIENCE

■ *Research Assistant,* 1994–1995, Aerospace Division, Rockwell, Seal Beach, CA. Member of team of computer scientists who evaluated test data on the performance of the Space Shuttle Orbiter designed and produced by Rockwell. Results will be used in design of electrical power system for space station.

■ *Research Associate,* 1995–present, Digital Data Processing, Massachusetts Institute of Technology, Lexington, MA. Researched systems for more efficient data reduction and analysis as well as improved algorithms for signal processing and analysis.

■ *Research Associate,* 1992–1994. Visual and Systems Interface, Cirrus Logic®, Fremont, CA. Assisted in research in the development of *2D/3D* graphics, video, and power management chips for both desktop and portable PCs.

WORK EXPERIENCE

■ *Consultant,* 1991–1993. Worldwide Information Services (WWIS), Unisys Corporation, Bismarck, ND. Advise clients in creative use and application of technology to improve service to customers, enhance their competitive position in their marketplace, and increase their flexibility.

■ *Visiting Assistant Professor,* 1990, Department of Computer Science, University of Hawaii, Honolulu, HI. Taught graduate courses in artificial intelligence, algorithms and theory, constructive logic, and computer graphics.

REFERENCES

Available upon request

Economics

CAXTON A. FABERSHAW, IV ——————————————————————— *Trade Representative*

Canadian Embassy-Apartado Mexico, D.F.
Tel: 555-2222; Fax: 555-0000

EXPERIENCE

- 1994–present   CANADIAN EMBASSY   1150 Mexico, D.F.

  Trade Representative. Negotiate, interpret, and implement Canadian trade policies and agreements of North American Free Trade Agreement (NAFTA); represent Canada in multilateral trade negotiations with Mexico and contiguous countries; prepare proposals for trade agreements that enhance profitability of Canadian trade in the hemisphere; advise Canadian firms of market opportunities in the region; supervise staff of thirty associates.

- 1990–1994   ROYAL BANK OF CANADA   Montréal (Québec)

  Economist. Multinational Banking Division. Analyzed and prepared annual reports on effectiveness of Investment and Corporate Divisions in delivering financial products to corporations, governments, and other major institutions around the world; prepared quarterly forecasts of trends in multinational banking.

- 1989–1990   THE INSTITUTE FOR RESEARCH   Montréal (Québec)
  ON PUBLIC POLICY

  L'Institut de Recherche en Politiques Publiques

  Senior Economic Consultant. Convened monthly focus groups composed of public and private sector executives in discussions of international trade and its impact on public policy; wrote monthly newsletter, which included economic analyses of policies and recommendations for implementation of innovative research programs; obtained $500,000 Canadian Economic Association grant for research on the impact of free enterprise zones on conservative public policies.

Caxton A. Fabershaw, IV _____ page two

AFFILIATIONS

The Conference Board of Canada
North Atlantic Council
        (Delegation of Canada to North Atlantic Council)
Organization of American States
        (Permanent mission of Canada to the Organizations of American States)
Canadian International Development Agency (CIDA)
British Columbia Chamber of Commerce
Musée d' art contemporian de Montréal

EDUCATION

• 1988   PRINCETON UNIVERSITY   Princeton, NJ (USA)

Postdoctoral studies in international economics

Coursework

Advanced Economic Theory	Econometric Modeling
Econometric Theory I, II	Public Finance
International Monetary Theory	International Trade Scale
Economics and Imperfect	
Competition Theory and Policy	

Research paper: "Factor Movements and Multinational Corporations"

• 1987   THE UNIVERSITY OF BRITISH COLUMBIA   Vancouver, BC

Ph.D. (High Honors) in economics

Major: International Economics

Dissertation: "Case Studies in Output and Price Determination in Open Economies"
Awarded J. Peter Norris Prize for Best Dissertation in International Economies

Courses in Economics

Empirical Research in Economics	Money and Banking
Economic History of Canada	International Economics
Labour Economics	Monetary Theory
International Macroeconomics	Econometric Analysis
Topics in Mathematical Economics	International Trade

Caxton A. Fabershaw, IV _____ page three

EDUCATION, cont'd

- 1984　　　　　　　　THE UNIVERSITY OF CALGARY　　　　　　　Calgary, Alberta

　　　　　　　　　　　B.Sc. (Honors) in psychology

　　Concentration:　　Experimental Psychology
　　Minor:　　　　　　Statistics

SKILLS

　　Languages:　　　　　Fluent in oral and written French, Spanish, and Portuguese
　　　　　　　　　　　　Conversant in oral German

　　Telecommunications:　Knowledge of UNIX; DOS environment; C Language; C++;
　　　　　　　　　　　　LAN/WAN
　　　　　　　　　　　　Communication protocols

　　Computer Networks:　ATM; VSAT; ISDN

PUBLICATIONS

- C. A. Fabershaw. "Myths and Mysteries of Corporate Debt." *The Economist.* 7947, 50–51, (1996).

- C. A. Fabershaw. "Investors and International Markets: An International Economics Perspective." *Fortune.* 133, 1, 60–63, (1996).

INTERESTS

Aboriginal affairs (treaty negotiations; management services; policy; planning, and research); Ojibway and Cree cultures; archery; chess; calligraphy

Spanish and Portuguese versions of this CV are available upon request.

German

JÜRGEN F. ALTSCHULER

---

2 Appian Way, East
Bloomington, IN 47426
(812) 555-4001
24-hour message: (812) 555-4711, ext. 29

office: (812) 555-1080, ext. 92
Fax: (812) 555-1087

BACKGROUND

Dual German-American citizenship with permanent residence in the United States of America. Past residence in Germany and Switzerland.

EDUCATION

STANFORD UNIVERSITY   Palo Alto, CA

Ph.D., 1990.   Major: Empires of the Mind: Nineteenth Century German Ideas. Topics in politics, religion, society, and history in the nineteenth century; Heine, Hegel, Schopenhauer, Feuerbach, Marx, Neitzsche, Burkhardt, Frisch, Rauke, D.F. Strauss, Tönnies, Weber, Freud.

Research Interests: Germanic linguistics and philology; foreign language pedagogy; theory of language; and computer assisted text analysis.

Dissertation, awarded high honors. Dissertation Review Committee, College of Arts and Sciences: "Psycholinguistic analysis of print advertisements for pediatric pharmaceuticals in popular journals, Federal Republic of Germany, 1991–1992."

WILLIAMS COLLEGE   Williamstown, MA

B.A., *summa cum laude,* 1985.

Major: German

Minor: computer science

Senior Thesis: "Schiller: Aesthetic Theory and Practice: The Nature and Function of the Artist and the Work of Art, in Schiller's Essays, Poetry, and Dramas"

JÜRGEN F. ALTSCHULER   - 2 -

HONORS AND AWARDS

Phi Beta Kappa, 1985, Williams College.
Goethe Prize for excellence in German language, 1985, Williams College.

FELLOWSHIPS

UNIVERSITY OF SOUTHERN CALIFORNIA   Los Angeles, CA

   1991 Andrew A. Mellon Postdoctoral Fellowship in the Humanities.

   Research: Theories of knowledge, language and the German Tradition.
                  Readings in Kant, Herder, Mauthner, Wittgenstein, Heidegger, and Habermas.

   Taught graduate courses on Wittgenstein and literary criticism.

UNIVERSITÄT MANNHEIM   Mannheim, Federal Republic of Germany

   1988   Deutscher Akademischer Austauschdienst, short-term research grant.

   Research: Foreign language pedagogy.

EXPERIENCE

INDIANA UNIVERSITY   Bloomington, IN

   1994   *Assistant Professor of German,* College of Arts and Sciences.

                 Taught advanced language courses and special topics in theories and history of
                 language, aesthetics, literature, and mythology. Team taught courses on computer
                 assisted text analysis.

DEUTSCHE GESELLSCHAFT FÜR AUSWÄRTIGE POLITIK, e. V.
                                             Bonn, Federal Republic of Germany

   1993   *Senior Researcher.* Areas of interest:
                 • The European Community: Progress or Decline.
                 • American foreign policy under change; the Middle East, and African Policy of
                   the U.S. since Carter.

INTERNATIONAL BUSINESS MACHINES   Frankfurt, Federal Republic of Germany

   1992   *Consultant,* Office of Communications and Global Markets.

SKILLS

Languages:

German:	Fluent (speak, read, write, translate, interpret)
Italian:	Conversationally fluent
French:	Conversationally fluent

Computer:

Programming languages: Java; C; C++; COBOL; Virtual Basic

Spread Sheet:

Excel

COMMUNITY SERVICE

Member, Ph.D. dissertation committees for D.K. Badenhausen (German language and literatures, 1991) and P.A. Koenig (Germanic linguistics and philology, 1996). Indiana University.

Faculty Advisor, Goethe Haus, living-learning residence for graduate students pursuing doctorate degrees in German language, 1994. Indiana University.

PRESENTATIONS

Altschuler, Jürgen F. "Fairy Tales as Literary Genre; Historic Relevance, types of Märchen from Volksmärchen to Kunstmärchen to the Anti-Märchen." Division on Teaching of Literature, MLA Convention. Atlanta, 28 December 1994.

Altschuler, Jürgen F. "Deutsche Kulturgeschichte." Association of German Nobility in North America, Triennial Meeting. Montreal, 1993.

Altschuler, Jürgen F., and Mueller, Max S. "The German Bildungsroman." German-American Chamber of Commerce, Symposium on "Culture and Enterprise." Chicago, 1992.

AFFILIATIONS

American Association of Teachers of German
Modern Language Association of America
American Philological Association
International Association of German Language and Literatures

Mathematics

SUJATA A. CHATTERJEE

8 Colonial Way, Morristown, NJ 07934 Fax: 201/555-6451   E-mail: schatterjee@aol.com   Tel: 201/555-471

BACKGROUND

Dual Indian and U.S.A. citizenship with extended residency in Sweden. Fluent in English, Hindi, Bengali, and Swedish. Superior skills in applied mathematics with particular emphasis on applications of mathematical and computer models for the development of effective management systems.

EXPERIENCE

AT&T BELL LABORATORIES
Morristown, NJ

1994–present

- *Senior Research Associate.* Manage team of twenty-five assistants in longitudinal study of the impact of short-term memory on effective management of hourly employees.

- *Systems Consultant.* Provided sales support, systems analysis and design, and presale management to ensure that solutions by AT&T match customers' systems.

- *Development Engineering Intern.* Assisted senior engineers in developing products and systems, in improving processes, and in conducting analyses.

TATA INSTITUTE OF FUNDAMENTAL RESEARCH
Bombay, India

1991

- *Assistant to Dr. V. R. Singh,* Director. Conducted research in pure and applied mathematics.

BOSE INSTITUTE
Calcutta, West Bengal

1990

- *Research Assistant* in nuclear physics and solid state physics.

BHABHA ATOMIC RESEARCH CENTRE
Bombay, India

1989

- *Assistant* to committee that studied the development of nuclear energy for peaceful purposes.

……………………………………………………………………………....................………………….... **2** ………Sujata A. Chatterjee

EDUCATION

MASSACHUSETTS INSTITUTE OF TECHNOLOGY
Cambridge, MA

Ph.D., 1994, *(cum laude)* in applied mathematics

Dissertation: "Linear partial differential operators in Gevrey spaces"[1]

Coursework:

-Ordinary and Partial Differential
-Theory of Functions of a Complex Variable
-Banach Algebras and Spectral Theory
-Unbounded Operations
-Classical Harmonic
-Transformation Groups

-Groups, Rings and Fields
-Ring Theory
-Representation Theory
-Homological Algebra
-Abstract Harmonic Analysis

UNIVERSITY OF CALCUTTA, Presidency College
West Bengal

M.Sc., 1990, in applied mathematics

Papers:

-K-theory
-Number theory
-Set theory
-Mathematical logic and foundations

-Geometry
-General topology
-Statistics
-Computer science

B.Sc., 1986, (First Class Honors) in mathematics

Pass subjects: physics and astronomy

SKILLS

Educational and practical knowledge of C; C11, UNIX; MS DOS Windows; networking technologies such as WAN, LAN, SNA, CPUs, JCL procedures; ES 9000; COBOL; PASCAL; X.400; X.25; SNA; OSI; database and design support software.

---

[1]Using Luigi Rodino's publication of the same title (River Edge, NJ: World Scientific Publishing Co., Inc., 1993).

....**3** ....Sujata A. Chatterjee

POSTDOCTORAL AWARDS AND STUDIES

The Mittag-Leffler Institute, 1991, Sweden
    Award: 100,000 Swedish crowns
    Studies: mathematical physics

The Lettie Delilah Hensen Fellowship at Rhodes University, 1990, Grahamstown, South Africa
    Studied pure and applied mathematics

AFFILIATIONS

Association for Symbolic Logic   Association for Women in Mathematics

PUBLICATIONS

S.A. Chatterjee. "Ordinary differential equations, partial differential equations, and applied
    mathematics" *Transactions of the American Mathematical Society,* **62** (1994), 172–194.

S.A. Chatterjee and Gifford von Edsel. "A UNIX tool for software development in determining
    executive compensation packages" *The Computer Journal* **27** (1995), 200–239.

S.A. Chatterjee and Mignon E. Delacroix. "Linear and multilinear algebra: some matrix theories"
    Studies in Applied Mathematics, **95** (1993), 6–18.

GRANTS

An empirical study of the impact of perceived environmental uncertainty and perceived agent effectiveness on the composition of compensation contracts. Research supported by a $50,000 grant from the National Science Foundation.

Some advanced technological and organizational implications for change in human resources management. Research supported by a $60,000 grant from AT&T Bell Laboratories.

Women's Studies

MAMIE FRAMPTON-GREEN

permanent:
1235 Central Ave.
Beaufort, SC 29902
(803) 555-1358
Fax: (803) 555-5902

office:
Congress Way and Main
Beaufort, SC 29902
(803) 555-3957
Fax: (803) 555-3958

PROFESSIONAL OBJECTIVE

To obtain a position as advisor to Governor Nancy Lee (R-LA) regarding women's issues

EDUCATION

Ph.D., 1992, in American History.

> Research interests: Transdisciplinary approaches to health care issues of affluent women in twentieth-century America: 1970–1990

M.A., 1987, Women's Studies, University of Wisconsin, Madison, WI.

> Thesis: "Oral histories of millionaire widows in Philadelphia, PA, Miami, FL, and Phoenix, AZ"

Coursework

Race, Class, and Gender
Gender and the Economy
Philosophy and Feminism
Latin-American Women Writers
African American Women Writers
Stratification Sociology

Field Methods in Oral History
Women's Health Issues
Women in American History
Corporate Finance
Accounting

B.A., *cum laude,* 1985, Fisk University, Nashville, TN.
Major in history; minor in natural sciences

> Senior thesis: "Images of affluent women in Pulitzer Prize winning fiction. 1960–1980"

EXPERIENCE

Director, City of Beaufort, Women's Resource Center, Beaufort, SC.

> Manage Center that provides family, personal, and career counseling, as well as public health services to professional women; supervise staff of eight including a clinical psychologist, financial planner, psychiatric social worker, and philosopher; manage budget of $400,000; generate 50% of budget from consultant services to government agencies and businesses. 1992–present.

MAMIE FRAMPTON-GREEN
page 2

EXPERIENCE (continued)

Assistant to Director of Community Relations, Bank of New England, Providence, RI.

> In cooperation with health care providers and insurers, developed community-based health care planning program for middle-income single mothers. 1989–1990.

Apprentice, Office of Hospital Administration, Nashville General Hospital, Nashville, TN.

> Assisted in assessing the quality of outpatient services for individuals suffering from acute fatigue syndrome; performed data entry using dBase 3. Summer 1987.

Intern, The Tennessee Historical Society, Nashville, TN.

> Edited catalog for centennial celebration. Summer 1986.

COMMUNITY SERVICE

Student Representative, Curriculum Committee, Women's Studies Department, University of Wisconsin—Madison. 1988–1989.

Volunteer, HELP-LINE, Nashville, TN. Provided counseling for troubled teens. 1989.

GRANTS

Recipient, American Friends of Cambridge Visiting Research Fellowship in the Arts, Cambridge University, Newham College, Cambridge, ENGLAND.

> Studied social science research methods, social psychology, and economics. 1990–1991.

Recipient, Alisha Sese Seko Travel Grant to Greece.

> Interviewed wives of prominent government officials. Wrote monograph for social science research course at Cambridge University. 1992.

AFFILIATIONS

National Women's Economic Alliance   •   American Historical Association   •   American Sociological Association

MAMIE FRAMPTON-GREEN
page 3

SKILLS

Leadership of groups committed to social change; facilitation of individual efforts toward achieving group objectives; motivation of individuals to achieve individual objectives; research; problem solving; observation of phenomena; critical judgments.

INTERESTS

Detective fiction; Hepplewhite furniture; bridge; chess; collector of vintage carburetors.

Architecture

Caesar Felipe Rodriquez II_____**Registered Architect**

residence:

261 Bloomfield
Otremont, Québec H2Y 1B6
514-555-2301

office:

11 Metcalf
Montréal, Québec H2Y 1B6
514-555-2796
Fax: 514-555-2783

Objective _____

To obtain a position with a licensed architectural consulting firm with client base in arts and entertainment, health care, higher education, and professional athletics.

Background _____

Dual Canadian/Portuguese citizenship with extensive residency in São Paulo, Brazil; Lisbon, Portugal; and Upper Sandusky, Ohio.

Experience _____

1992–present   Rodriquez & Rodriquez, Architects   Montréal, Québec

Partner

- Draft and design multibuilding complexes for the public domain such as college campuses, residential communities, hospitals, nursing homes, and entertainment centres

- Supervise staff of five associates

- Arrange client presentations

- Assist clients in obtaining construction proposals

1991–1992   Ministère de L'Environnement   Montréal, Québec

Associate Architect

- Assisted in preparation of architectural documents and drawings

- Researched municipal building codes and materials

- Wrote specifications for building materials

Summers 1990, 1991   Ministère du Tourisme   Québec City, Québec

Assistant Architect

- Developed cost figures for construction and maintenance of facilities

- Prepared drawings, specifications, and related construction documents for facilities

Caesar Felipe Rodriquez II_____ 2 _____

Education _____

1991 **M.Sc. A**   Université de Montréal   Montréal, Québec
                   École d' Architecture
                   Faculté de l'Amenagement

Design thesis (awarded high honours): Schematic design of biosphere using alternative sources of energy, materials, and construction techniques.

Coursework

- CONCEPTS D'SPACE
- RAPPORTS PERSONNE-SOCIETE-ENVIRONNEMENT
- LE DESIGN DEPUIS 1960
- INTEGRATION DE L'ARCHITECTURE AU MILIEU
- METHODES DE RESTAURATION
- LABORATOIRE D'ARCHITECTURE
- LE LABORATOIRE D'ACOUTIQUE
- LE LABORATOIRE DE CLIMATOLOGIE ET D'ENERGIE
- LE LABORATOIRE D'INFORMATIQUE

1989 **B Arch**   Université de Laval à Québec   Québec City, Québec
                  École d'Architecture

Skills _____

- Fluent in English, Portuguese, and French (oral and written; writing proficiency in all three languages)
- Strong background and experience in
  —physical sciences
  —humanities
- Detailed knowledge of and practical experience in design
- Proficient in use of computer-assisted design techniques

Professional Associations _____

- Order des architects du Québec
- The Royal Architectural Institute of Canada
- Society for the Study of Architecture in Canada

Portfolio _____

Portfolio, references, and transcripts available upon request

A French version of this CV is available upon request.

Business

curriculum vitae

JOSEPH GERONIMO GIST
(Sequoya)

Offices

•Rockefeller Center
Suite 6126
New York, NY 10004
Tel: (212)555-8091
Fax: (212) 555-8937
E-mail: jggist@aol.com

•Villa Roma Ippolito
Via Grassi 10
20122 Milano
ITALY
Tel. 243689
E-mail: gist@oasi.milano.it

Experience

CHEROKEE INTERNATIONAL MARKETING, INC.
New York, NY and Milan, Italy

President and Chief Executive Officer 1992–present

- Manage $50,000,000 international marketing firm, which specializes in providing services for major manufacturers of consumer products

- Firm employs 3,000 worldwide

- Increased profits 25% (1994) and 35% (1995)

- Increased clients by 50% (1993); very effective in creating client loyalty

- Board of Directors has approved plan for opening offices in Barcelona, Frankfurt, London, and Toronto

PROCTER & GAMBLE
Rome, Italy and Dublin, Ireland

Vice President, Marketing European Division 1988–1992

- Implemented marketing strategies for detergents, soft drinks, and pharmaceuticals

- Managed staff of 125, representing diverse cultural and linguistic backgrounds

COCA-COLA FOODS DIVISION
Atlanta, GA and Caracas, Venezuela

Assistant Vice President, Sales and Marketing 1984–1988

- Developed and implemented sales/marketing strategy for emerging international markets

- Supervised staff of 200 sales personnel in Caracas

JOSEPH GERONIMO GIST

Skills

- Strong conceptualization, analytical, and interpersonal skills essential for administration of an international corporation

- Proven success in motivating colleagues and staff, as well as promoting teamwork

- Significant experience and expertise in developing and implementing sales and marketing strategies particularly for international markets

- Fluent in Italian, Spanish, and German

Education

- NORTHWESTERN UNIVERSITY, Evanston, IL   1982–1984
  MBA The J.L. Kellogg Graduate School of Management
  Specialty: international marketing

Coursework

- International Business Management
- International Marketing II
  - Cross-cultural issues in International Management
- International and Foreign Marketing
- International Marketing Management

- UNIVERSITA DEGLI STUDI DI million, Milano, Italy   1979
  Fulbright Scholar. Studied economics and international affairs

- CORNELL UNIVERSITY, Ithaca, NY   1976–1978
  BA, *cum laude,* Native American Studies
  minor: economics and international relations

  Activities:

  - *President,* Class of 1978

  - *Co-captain,* Varsity Lacrosse, 1977, 1978

  - *President,* Alpha Omega Psi Fraternity, 1977

Affiliations

- American Marketing Association
- Sales and Marketing Executives International
- Marketing Research Association
- National Congress of American Indians
- League of the Six-Iroquois Nations in New York State and Canada
- The Pre-Columbian Powhattan Confederacy—East Coast
- The All-Pueblo Council in the Southwest

Interests

Native American languages, history, art, and music   •   Italian Renaissance opera and dance

Engineering

CHAUNCEY MERRILL THIGPEN

Professional Engineer_____

4 Landsdowne Court, Houston, TX 77008 • 713/555-2222 (messages)
Fax: 713/555-0000 • E-mail: cthigpen.air.com

OBJECTIVE

A chemical engineering position in project development, including equipment specification, procurement, cost control, project scheduling, and installation

EXPERIENCE

Project Engineer, Air Liquide, Houston, TX   1993–present
    Supervise industrial gas technology team of ten chemical engineers in development and production of oxygen, nitrogen, and carbon dioxide

Process Engineer, PPG Industries, Pittsburgh, PA   1992–1993
    Researched impact of production of chlorine caustic soda on sub-tropical environments

Hoescht Celanese, Somerville, NJ   1990–1992

  Researcher   Developed specialty chemicals for Crayola® Crayons

  Associate Chemist Monitored tests of pigments used in Tupperware and Rubbermaid products

  Assistant Chemist Monitored tests of printing inks for *National Geographic Magazine*

ENGINEERING REGISTRATIONS

Fundamentals of Engineering Examination   1986

Principles of Practice of Engineering Education, Texas   1995

EDUCATION

Ph.D., University of Minnesota, Minneapolis, MN   1991

    Major: chemical engineering

    Dissertation: "Case studies in the use of photogrammetry in retrofit projects"

    Coursework: • Computational Methods in Chemical Engineering and Material Science

             • Principles of Chemical Engineering

             • Unit Operations and Separation Processes

             • Scientific Models for Engineering Processes

two_____Chauncey Merrill Thigpen

Coursework: • Advanced Mathematics for Chemical Engineers

(cont'd)   • Physical and Chemical Thermodynamics

               • Chemical Reaction Kinetics—Kinetics of Homogeneous Reactions

               • Chemical Reaction Analysis

               • Chemical Engineering Laboratory

               • Process Evaluation and Design

               • Process Control

               • Research in Chemical Engineering

B.Sc., University of Illinois at Urbana-Champaign, Urbana, IL   1986

      Major: chemical engineering

PRESENTATION

"Refinery Optimization Using Total Site (Pinch) Technology and Simulation Specification Data Sheets," CHEMPUTERS, Conference and Exhibition of Computer Technology for Chemical Engineers, Houston, TX, 14, 15 February 1996.

PUBLICATIONS

C. M. Thigpen, "Process simulation. The art and science of modeling. A powerful engineering tool," *Chemical Engineering,* 101, 10, 82 (1994).

Thigpen, Chauncey M. *Catalytic Liquid Phase Hydrogenation.* New York: McGraw-Hill, 1995.

SKILLS/ABILITIES

Technical: LANs; WANs; client-server, object-oriented; C++; Visual BASIC; COBOL; NonStop SQL; TCP/IP; OLTP; UNIX; POSIX; MS DOS Windows

Highly developed teamwork abilities; superior communication, leadership, and flexibility skills

AFFILIATIONS

American Chemical Society   American Institute of Chemical Engineers

REFERENCES

Available upon request

General Medicine

GENEVIEVE MARGARET ACKERMAN, M.D.

Director, University Health Services
University of Montana
Missoula, MT 59812
Tel: (406) 555-7906
Fax: (406) 555-8291
E-mail: gackerman@uiuc.edu

SPECIALTY

General and Family Practice
Subspecialty: community health

EDUCATION

- BROWN UNIVERSITY   Providence, RI
    M.D. 1986 Program in Medicine
        Clerkships:
        -Acute care   Roger Williams General Hospital   Providence, RI
        -Pediatrics   The Emma Pendleton Bradly Hospital   Providence, RI

- DARTMOUTH MEDICAL SCHOOL   Hanover, NH
    1984 The Brown-Dartmouth Program in Medical Education

Coursework

Year I		Year II	
Anatomy	Microbiology	Psychiatry	Epidemiology
Biochemistry	Neuroscience	Pharmacology	Clinical History
Cell Biology	Pathology	Physical Diagnosis	
Human Genetics	Physiology	The Scientific Basis of Medicine	

- BRYN MAWR COLLEGE   Bryn Mawr, PA
    1983 Post-baccalaureate Pre-medical Program

- UNIVERSITY OF MISSOURI—COLUMBIA   Columbia, MO
    1979 A.B.   *magna cum laude*
    Major: anthropology
    Minor: journalism

Honor: **Phi Beta Kappa**

CERTIFICATION and LICENSURE

- 1991 Medical License, State of Missouri

- 1990 Medical License, State of Missouri

- 1985 American Board of Family Practice

- 1964 Diplomate, National Board of Medical Examiners

-2-   **GENEVIEVE MARGARET ACKERMAN, M.D.**

- UNIVERSITY OF NEVADA   Reno, NV
    1990 School of Medicine
        Internship in community health

- UNIVERSITY OF NEBRASKA   Omaha, NE
    1987 College of Medicine
        Residency in general and family practice

- GEORGE WASHINGTON UNIVERSITY   Washington, DC
    1988–1989 School of Medicine and Health Services
        Residency in internal medicine

EXPERIENCE

- UNIVERSITY OF MONTANA   Missoula, MT
    1994–present *Director,* University Health Services

- UNIVERSITY OF NORTH DAKOTA   Grand Rapids, ND
    School of Medicine
    1994–present *Visiting Assistant Professor*

- NBC NEWS   New York, NY
    1993–1994 *Research Assistant to Health Sciences Correspondent*

- NEW ENGLAND JOURNAL OF MEDICINE   Waltham, MA
    1992–1994 *Associate Editor*

AFFILIATIONS

- American Academy of Family Physicians

- American Medical Association

- National Association of Medical Writers

INTERESTS

- Scientific writing (medical); Go; white water rafting; Mayan art; needlepoint; kickboxing

Law

PIERCE S. STATLER III
Suite 1200, Carnegie Towers
1777 Fifth Avenue
Pittsburgh, PA 15275

Residence: 412-555-1921

Office: 412-555-0923

Fax: 412-555-5883

Fax: 412-555-1801

E-mail: pstatler@cros.net

Member of the Bar: State of West Virginia, admitted 1990
State of Pennsylvania, admitted 1991

EDUCATION

WEST VIRGINIA UNIVERSITY, College of Law   Morgantown, WV
Juris Doctorate, June 1990

Honors and Awards: Order of the Coif
Roger Douglas, Jr. Memorial Prize for highest
first year GPA West Virginia Bar Merit Scholarship

Activities:
Editor, West Virginia University Law Review, 1988–1989
Editorial Assistant, National Coal Issue, Eastern Mineral Law Foundation, Inc., 1987
Member   Moot Court Board, 1986
Intellectual Property Association
Phi Alpha Delta

UNIVERSITY OF OXFORD, Balliol College   Oxford, England
Rhodes Scholar
M. Phil., 1986
Course: economics
Activities: crew, football, debate

WEST VIRGINIA UNIVERSITY   Morgantown, WV
B.A., *summa cum laude,* 1986. Major in economics (GPA 4.0); minor in English
and international studies. Cumulative GPA 4.0.

Academic Awards:
Phi Beta Kappa
Omicron Delta Epsilon, national honorary society in economics

PIERCE S. STATLER III

-2-

LEGAL EXPERIENCE

SUPREME COURT OF THE UNITED STATES   Washington, DC

Law Clerk.   Honorable Sandra Day O'Connor. Performed duties such as research, drafting, editing, proofreading, and verification of citations; drafted working opinions pursuant to her direction. 1989–1990.

LTV STEEL COMPANY   Pittsburgh, PA

Attorney.   Legal Department. Manage staff of ten; expedite international legal matters of multinational corporation such as anti-dumping and countervailing duty laws; import exclusion proceedings and export licensing; bilateral trade agreements; and treaties and foreign laws. 1994–present.

GOODWIN & GOODWIN   Charlestown, WV

Associate.   Researched and drafted memoranda concerning corporate matters vis-à-vis banking and commercial law; managed team of four associates who prepared briefs for public utilities seeking redress in labor issues. 1991–1993.

PUBLIC DEFENDER CORPORATION   Moundsville, WV

Consultant.   Provided representation in consumer law. 1990.

PUBLICATIONS

International Trade and Protectionist Economies, 20 *Yale L.J.* 503 (1991).

Most Favored Nation Legislation and Free Market Economies, *18 Stan. J. Int. L.* 339 (1992).

The Human Rights Conundrum, Political Expedience, and International Trade, 10 *W. Virginia L. Rev.* 6 (1994).

SKILLS SUMMARY

Expert oral and written communication skills; practical experience in administration, supervision, negotiation, teaching, training, and tutoring.

AFFILIATIONS

AMERICAN BAR ASSOCIATION   Chicago, IL

Young Lawyers Division.
Chairperson. International Law Committee, 1994.

PENNSYLVANIA BAR ASSOCIATION   Pittsburgh, PA

WEST VIRGINIA BAR ASSOCIATION   Charlestown, WV

INTERESTS

Crew; physical fitness; music (Gregorian Chants); Impressionist painting.

Higher Education

ACY L. JACKSON
918 Rutherford Lane
Pemberville, OH 44532

HOME: (419) 555-7752
OFFICE: (419) 555-4010, ext. 410
ajackson@msn.com

EDUCATION

Invited Participant *(one of three Americans), International Seminar on Career Planning and Placement, Oxford University, Oxford, England, Fall 1990.*

Participant, *Institute for Educational Management, Harvard University, Cambridge, MA, Summer 1985.*

M.A., *Teaching English as a Foreign Language, Teachers College, Columbia University, New York, NY, 1970. Awarded Departmental Assistantship with Dr. Edward J. Cervenka, Distinguished Professor of Bilingual Education.*

M.Ed., *Religious Education and Counseling, University of Pittsburgh, Pittsburgh, PA, 1964. University of Tehran, Tehran, Iran. Studied Middle Eastern Culture, History and Religion with Dr. Seyed Hussein Nasr, 1967–1968.*

B.B.A., *Economics and Business Administration, Westminster College, New Wilmington, PA, 1958. Elected to* Who's Who in American Colleges and Universities.

ADMINISTRATION

Principal, *Acy L. Jackson & Associates, Management Consulting Firm, Hamilton, NY 1994, 1995 and Owens Mills, MD 1995–1997.*

Co-Director, *Office of Intercultural Resources, Colgate University, Hamilton, NY, 1993–1995.*

- *Developed syllabus for course, "Understanding Culture and Cultures Through Intercultural Sensitivity, Communication, and Effectiveness." Taught portion of course as model at St. Lawrence University's and Association of American Colleges and Universities' national conferences, "Teaching Cultural Encounters as General Education," March 1995, New Orleans.*

- *Co-managed $95,000 annual budget of three-year grant from Fund for the Improvement of Postsecondary Education (FIPSE), U.S. Department of Education.*

- *Facilitated reentry workshops for students returning from study abroad.*

Director, *Career Planning Center, Colgate University, 1978–1993.*

- *Supervised staff of nineteen—four assistant directors, three secretaries, and twelve students.*

- *Planned, implemented, and coordinated seminars, workshops, counseling and referral services, and dissemination of career information to faculty, staff, students, and representatives of employing institutions, and graduates and professional schools.*

- *Planned, implemented, and coordinated job fairs with institutions such as Amherst, Bowdoin, Brown, Colby, Dartmouth, Georgetown, Stanford, Tufts, in Boston, Chicago, New York, and Washington, DC.*

Associate Dean of Students, *Colgate University, 1985–1993.*

- *Ex-officio member, Graduate Fellowship Committee, Colgate University, 1978–1992. Advised and counseled students applying for Mellon, Fulbright, Rhodes, Marshall, Watson, Churchill, and St. Andrew's fellowships, scholarships, and grants; served as campus liaison with above sponsors; prepared credentials of applicants for review by Committee.*

Assistant Dean for Supportive Services, *Colgate University, 1983–1985.*

- *Supervised professional staff of seven, including Director of Writing Program and Director of Math Clinic.*

- *Managed budget of $985,000.*

- *Developed guidelines for university-wide tutoring program.*

ADMINISTRATION
(continued)

Associate Dean of Students, *The College of Wooster, OH, 1972–1978.*

- *Counseled and guided students in personal, education, and career concerns.*

Director, *Career Planning and Placement Service, The College of Wooster, 1972–1978.*

- *Administered career development program for liberal arts students, faculty, alumni, administrators, and representatives of employing institutions.*

- *Designed and facilitated workshops such as Life Planning, Decision Making, New Directions (career exploration), Logistics of the Job Search, and Graduate and Professional Education.*

Director/Consultant, *Armaghan English Language Institute, Tehran, Iran, 1970–1972.*

- *Administered English language teaching programs for 500 students each of three quarters; coordinated instructional efforts under the aegis of Iranian Ministries of Education and Higher Education and the United Presbyterian Church (USA); supervised six full-time and eight part-time teachers, and four administrators.*

INSTRUCTION

Member, *Adjunct Faculty Owens Community College, Toledo, OH, Spring 2001–present. Composition instruction and curriculum and course development.*

Member, *Adjunct Faculty Terra Community College, Fremont, OH, 1998–present. Developmental Writing instruction.*

WSOS, *Fremont, OH, Summer 1998. Designed and conducted workshops on job-seeking skills for teenagers in Sandusky, Wood, Ottawa, and Seneca Counties.*

Instructor/Facilitator, *The College of Lake County, Grayslake, IL, August 1995. Conducted faculty development workshop on intercultural sensitivity, communication, and effectiveness; advised senior staff on developing guidelines for global studies course.*

Instructor, *English Language Institute, Syracuse University, Syracuse, NY, Summers 1986–1991. Taught English conversation, writing, listening, and grammar to graduate students from yearly average of eighteen countries.*

Instructor-at-Large, *The College of Wooster, Wooster, OH, 1974–1978. Taught special problem courses developed in response to student interests; Freshman Colloquium, with major focus on writing, personal and academic adjustment, and skill development; career development course for students planning careers in teaching.*

English Teacher and Director of Cocurricular Programs, *The Alborz Foundation, Tehran, Iran, 1965–1968. Taught advanced conversation classes and beginning classes in oral-aural English; developed format for and implementation of seminars and discussions regarding cultural issues.*

English Teacher, *C.T.I. High School, Sialkot, West Pakistan, 1958–1961. Taught high school students reading, writing, speaking, and listening skills in preparation for government examinations.*

COURSE DEVELOPMENT AND COURSE INSTRUCTION

Courses developed: Colgate University   *"Understanding Culture and Cultures Through Intercultural Sensitivity, Communication, and Effectiveness"*

COURSE DEVELOPMENT AND COURSE INSTRUCTION
(continued)

Courses developed:	*Terra Community College*	*British Literature II* *Victorian Period* *"The Short Story"* *"Writing Historical Fiction"* *"Write an Heirloom"*
Courses taught:	*ESL* * Syracuse University*	*Teaching English as a Foreign* * Language*
	Developmental Education * Terra Community College*	*Eng 081, Developmental* * Writing/Grammar* *Eng 085, Reading*
	Owens Community College	*Eng 101, The Writing Process*
	English	*Eng 105, College Composition I* *Eng 106, College Composition II*
	ElderCollege * Terra Community College*	*"The Short Story"* *"Writing Historical Fiction"* *"Write an Heirloom"*
	ElderVision * Lourdes College*	*"Write an Heirloom"*

PUBLICATIONS

Author, How to Prepare Your Curriculum Vitae, *Lincolnwood, IL: VGM Horizons, 1992. Second edition was released October 1996; currently writing third edition for publication with McGraw-Hill in Spring 2003.*

Author, *"The Conversation Class,"* English Teaching Forum, *vol. VIII (January–February, 1969), No. 1, 19–20. Reprinted in* Die Unterrichtsproaxis, *2.2, F 1969. Reprinted in* English Teaching Forum, *Special Issue, vol. XIII, 1975.*

Author, *"Career Counseling for Minority Persons," in* Career Development in the 1980's: Theory and Practice, *Springfield, IL: Charles C. Thomas, 1981.*

Career Counselor, *"Life's Work: Four Approaches to Career Counseling," produced by Career Services, Radcliffe College, and Cambridge Documentary Films, Cambridge, MA, 1992. One of four prominent career counselors who conducted session with same client. Referred to as ". . . defining film of the profession."*

CONSULTATION

Faculty Handbook Committee, *compilation of vital information to assist new full-time and part-time faculty, Terra Community College, September 1998–May 1999.*

Head, Evaluation Team, *Office of Career Development and Resources, Wesleyan University, Middletown, CT, 1982.*

Chairman, *Eastern College Personnel Officers Visitation Team, University of Massachusetts-Boston, Boston, MA, 1985.*

Consultant, *professors and administrators regarding research, material development, teacher training and design of courses of study in learning and instruction in English as a Foreign Language at American University of Beirut, Beirut College for Women, and International College all in Beirut, Lebanon; The Regional English Language Centre, Singapore; Tokyo's Women's Christian College, Tokyo, Japan; and the University of Hawaii, Honolulu, Hawaii, 1972.*

CONSULTATION
(continued)

Consultant/Member, *Distinguished Faculty, American Management Association, New York, NY, 1978–1984; 1990; 1992. Facilitated and instructed Life Planning Workshops for Operation Enterprise Program.*

AWARDS

Who's Who Among America's Teachers, *"The Best Teachers in America Selected by the Best Students," 2000.*

President's Club, *HECHT's, Owings Mills, MD. One of twenty-two sales associates whose production accounted for 11% of $30,000,000 in sales for 1997.*

Diamond Star, *HECHT's, Owings, Mills, MD. Highest award for friendliness to customers in a selling season; i.e., three exceptionally friendly mystery shopper observations or two exceptionally friendly mystery shopper observations and one customer commendation, 1998, 1997.*

Outstanding Full-time Employee, *Polo Ralph Lauren, HECHT's, Owings Mills, MD, 1998.*

Silver Medal Award *for alumni service to Colgate University. Council for Advancement and Support of Education, 1987.*

Administrative Development Award, *Colgate University, 1985.*

COMMUNICATION SKILLS

Language:	*Fluent*
	• *English*
	Conversationally fluent
	• *Persian*
	Conversationally proficient
	• *Urdu*
Communication:	*Excellent*
	• *Oral and written skills*
	• *Interpersonal skills*
	• *Organizational skills*
Computer:	*Familiar with*
	• *Windows 95, 97, 2000*
	• *MS Office*
	• *MS Word*
	• *PowerPoint*
	• *Excel*

Composition and Rhetoric

C. KATHLEEN GECKEIS
635 Walnut Street
Perrysburg, OH 44320

HOME: (419) 555-2660
OFFICE: (419) 555-3472
E-MAIL: kgeckeis@owens.edum

EDUCATION

Master of Arts Degree, English Literature, emphasis on Composition and Rhetoric, *the University of Toledo, Toledo, OH, September 1996–June 1997.*

***Composition
and Rhetoric:***

- *Teaching of Composition, Part I*
- *Teaching of Composition, Part II*
- *The Composing Process I: Computer-Assisted Instruction, Rhetorical Invention Strategies and Portfolio Writing*
- *The Composing Process II: Peer Response and Technical Writing*
- *Current Composition Theory*

Literature:

- *Restoration Literature*
- *Renaissance Literature*
- *Early Romanticism*
- *Post-modernism*
- *Unruly Women: Women Who Rule: 16th and 17th Century Literature*
- *Bibliography and Research Methods*

Linguistics:

- *Introduction to Linguistics*
- *History of the English Language*

Master of Arts Degree, German Language, Literature, and Translation, *Kent State University, Kent, OH, 1990.*

Baccalaureate of Arts Degree in German, *Kent State University, Kent, OH, 1988.*

INSTRUCTION

Adjunct English Instructor, *Owens Community College, Toledo, OH, instruction of composition, developmental writing, and German courses, 1996–PRESENT.*

Writing:
- *Developmental Writing 101*
- *College Composition I*
- *College Composition II*

German:
- *Elementary German I*
- *Elementary German II*

Adjunct English Instructor, *Terra State Community College, Fremont, OH, instruction, curriculum development, and course development, 1992–2000.*

Composition and Literature:
- *Modern American Novel*
- *Introduction to Short Fiction*
- *College Composition I*
- *College Composition II*
- *Business and Technical Writing*

Developmental Education:
- *Developmental Writing*
- *Reading Comprehension*

INSTRUCTION
(continued)

Humanities:
- Humanities 101: Critical Thinking
- Introduction to Humanities

International Trade:
- Cultural Awareness for International Trade

German:
- Elementary German I, II, III
- Intermediate German I
- Intermediate German II: Introduction to Literature
- Intermediate German III: Introduction to Business German

Graduate Assistant, Carlson Library, University of Toledo, August 1995–June 1996

- Instruction of library skills
- Instruction of OhioLINK databases

German Instructor and Graduate Assistant, Kent State University, August 1987–May 1990

Instructor of English as a Second Language, the Federal Republic of Germany, November 1980–May 1986

COURSE DEVELOPMENT

Developmental Writing:

- Developmental Writing 101, developed and piloted course that incorporated writing center pedagogy and one-to-one conferencing techniques.

Composition:

- College Composition I
- College Composition II

German:

- Elementary German, I, II, III

German:

- Intermediate German I
- Intermediate German II: Introduction to Literature
- Intermediate German III: Introduction to German Business Writing

International Trade:

- Cultural Awareness for International Trade

ADMINISTRATION

Manager, the Writing Centers, Toledo and Findlay Campuses, Owens Community College, January 2000–PRESENT.

- Supervise staff of 25+
- Train writing mentors in writing center, developmental writing, and ESL pedagogies
- Hold conferences with composition, developmental writing, and ESL students

ADMINISTRATION
(continued)

- *Hold writing assignment design workshops for faculty*
- *Conduct Teaching and Learning Forum*
- *Develop Writing Across the Curriculum Program*
- *Hire writing mentors and student workers*
- *Evaluate writing mentors and student workers*
- *Purchase materials, supplies, and equipment for Writing Centers*
- *Process payroll*

LEADERSHIP EXPERIENCE

Chair, Teaching and Learning Forum, *Owens Community College, 2000–PRESENT.*

Editor, Write Now, *Writing Center Newsletter, Owens Community College, 2000–PRESENT.*

Editor, Speaking of Learning . . . , *Teaching and Learning Newsletter, Owens Community College, 2001–PRESENT.*

Co-editor, Honestly, *Writer's Workshop Publication, Owens Community College, 2000–PRESENT.*

IEP Grant Award, *$1,200 to publish* The Journal of World Language Poetry and Prose: Original and Translated Literary Works, *Spring 2000.*

Faculty Handbook Development Committee, *compilation of vital information to assist new full-time and part-time faculty, Terra Community College, September 1998–December 1999.*

Writing Center Tutor, *Terra Community College, provided students with help in all areas of writing and rhetorical strategies; taught students to become independent thinkers and critical thinkers, September 1997–December 1999.*

Community College Core Curriculum Committee, *curriculum development, Spring 1995.*

Project Proposal for Improving Foreign Language Education, *sponsored by the American Association of Community Colleges: set forth strategies for foreign-language faculty development, workshops, and curriculum development, Fall 1993.*

Informal supervision of foreign-language faculty, *January 1992–September 1993.*

International Trade Technologies Program Advisory Committee, *curriculum and course development, August 1991–September 1993.*

Graduate Committee Representative, *represented graduate student concerns, August 1988–May 1990.*

Graduate Student Senate Representative, *communication of available funds, programs, and services to German department. Funds received purchased various texts, dictionaries, German films, and literary works for departmental archives, August 1987–May 1988.*

PROFESSIONAL ORGANIZATIONS

- *Ohio Association of Developmental Education (2000–PRESENT)*
- *National Association of Developmental Education (2000–PRESENT)*
- *NCTE (2000–PRESENT)*
- *International Writing Centers Association (2000–PRESENT)*
- *Delta Phi Alpha, National German Honorary (1988–PRESENT)*
- *American Translators' Association (1989–1990)*
- *North Ohio Translators' Association (1988–1990)*
- *American Association of Teachers of German (1987–1990)*

ACHIEVEMENTS, AWARDS, AND NOMINATIONS

- *IEP Grant for $1,200 to publish* The Journal of World Language Poetry and Prose: Original and Translated Literary Works
- *Editor of* Write Now, *Writing Center Newsletter*
- *Editor of* Speaking of Learning . . . *Teaching and Learning Newsletter*
- *Co-editor of* Honestly, *Writers' Workshop Publication*
- *Two-year Graduate Tuition Remission Scholarship, University of Toledo, English Department*
- *Mortar Board Award for Academic Achievement*
- *Ester L. Grant Award for Academic Achievement, Highest GPA*
- *Nomination for the David B. Smith Fellowship, Outstanding Graduate Student*
- *Certificate of Advanced Proficiency in German, the "Goethe Institut" Grade: "sehr gut" (excellent)*
- *Three-year Tuition Remission Scholarship, Kent State University, German Department*

PUBLICATIONS AND PRESENTATIONS

Jackson, Acy L., and C. Kathleen Geckeis. How to Prepare Your Curriculum Vitae, *with McGraw-Hill for publication in Spring 2003.*

Assessing Factors That Influence the Content of Conference Reports: Stating Clear Objectives and Outcomes. *Presentation at the International Writing Centers Association Conference in Savannah, GA. April 11, 2002.*

COMMUNICATION SKILLS

LANGUAGES: Fluent

- *English*
- *German*

Two years

- *College Spanish*

COMMUNICATION: Excellent

- *Oral and written skills*
- *Interpersonal skills*
- *Organizational skills*

COMPUTER: Familiar with

- *Microsoft Word*
- *Microsoft Works*
- *Windows 95, 97, 2000*
- *PowerPoint*
- *Internet*
- *OhioLINK Databases*

The Electronic Curriculum Vitae

In keeping with the bold innovations in telecommunications, a revolution of monumental proportions is occurring in the job-search process. While recent developments are having a profound impact on the way major corporations first screen applicants for positions, the ripple effects are being felt not only by prospective employers in small- to medium-sized organizations but also in the ways in which individuals prepare information to present themselves as applicants for positions. The revolution involves computers, which have now set the standards by which information is processed and presented to decision makers.

As you prepare your curriculum vitae and its accompanying correspondence, use the samples in Chapters 4 and 5 as guidelines. It is essential that you prepare at least two copies of your material: one for individuals to read and one to be scanned by a computer. To determine whether to send the scannable or nonscannable CV, query admissions officers and contacts at employing institutions. Suggestions are also often found in advertisements. Not surprisingly, the computer drives the new technology, defines the terms, and sets the structure and guidelines for the information it will reject. Traditionally, for example, hiring professionals expected applicants to use action verbs to describe what they had done or could do. In the new mode, individuals are required to use nouns or job titles, as computers are programmed to scan CVs for certain prescribed ideal characteristics in applicants. These nouns or ideal characteristics are called keywords. In scannable résumés and CVs, these words appear in prescribed positions at the beginning of the document.

Several publications have anticipated and essentially defined this electronic revolution. Two such publications are:

Kennedy, Joyce Lain, and Thomas J. Morrow. *The Electronic Resume Revolution.* 2nd ed. New York: John Wiley & Sons, 1995.

Kennedy, Joyce Lain, and Thomas J. Morrow. *The Electronic Job Search Revolution.* New York: John Wiley & Sons, 1994.

Several features define the ideal scannable curriculum vitae. As you create a scannable CV, focus on clearly defined format and content rules, which are determined by Optical Character Recognition (OCR). These rules create a text file in ASCII (American Standard Code for Information Interchange). Next, artificial intelligence reads the text and extracts the information it needs. Therefore, use clean, crisp, and dark type—preferably standard fonts—so that OCR can recognize every letter. Include specific keywords when describing your skills, education, and experience. Use language and acronyms that are appropriate for the field in which you are seeking entry. Be succinct. Use commonly accepted headings such as all capitalization for the sections and active verbs when noting responsibilities and skills. Do not be concerned about length, as the computer's ability to scan is not affected by it.[1]

---

[1]Adapted from "Preparing the Ideal Scannable Resume." Resumix Corporation, 1995.

Tips for Producing a Scannable Curriculum Vitae

_____ Produce a letter-quality original.

_____ Use a standard typeface in a font size of 12 to 14 points.

_____ Avoid using italics, underlining, lines, graphics, two-column format, or boxes. Emphasize text using boldface type or full capitalization.

_____ Use standard spacing; letters should not touch.

_____ Place your name at the top of the first page, followed by your address on the next line. Include your phone number on a separate line.

_____ Place your name as the first text on each successive page.

_____ Do not fold or staple, and use a manila envelope.

Sample Scannable Curricula Vitae

The format and design of the following scannable CVs adhere to guidelines established by Joyce Lain Kennedy and Thomas J. Morrow in their pioneering publication, *Electronic Resume Revolution.*

MOIRA ELSPETH SOAMES

Big Sky Ranch • Jackson Hole, WY 82072 • 307 765-6029
maisonette theasthai • Savannah, GA 31401 • 912 262-0015
Messages: 912 267-0000
E-Mail: soames@yahoo.com

KEYWORD PROFILE Actress. Toy Designer. Producer. Writer. Cartoonist. Film Maker. Dancer. Fund-raiser. Suburban Teens. Substance Abuse. Fitness. Dependability. Mature Judgment. High Energy. Creative. Flexible. Sensitive. Competitive. Detail-Minded. Public Speaking. Organizational Skills. Results-Oriented. Team Player. Ensemble. MFA Degree. BFA Degree. University of Wisconsin—Madison. Video Production. West Virginia University. Professional Diploma in Film Production. Presidential Scholar in the Arts. University Scholar. National Endowment for the Arts Administrative Fellows Program.

OBJECTIVE   A fund-raising position for ensemble productions of documentaries depicting quality fitness and nutrition programs for suburban teens engaged in substance abuse

EXPERIENCE

1994–Present   **Production Intern/Assistant Development Officer.** The American Place Theatre. New York, NY. Assisted production manager in rehearsals and running of productions; solicited corporate foundations for financial support of theatre productions; raised $95,000 for annual theatre summer festival productions

1992–1994   **Associate Stage Manager/Public Relations Specialist.** Circle Repertory Company, New York, NY. Managed development projects; supervised backstage crew of eighteen; assisted stage manager in twelve productions; made monthly appearances on public television to solicit funds for theatre productions

1991–1992   **Assistant Literary/Dramaturg.** The Guthrie Theatre, Minneapolis, MN. Researched backgrounds for productions; wrote reviews of theatre productions

Summer 1991   **Production Assistant.** Castillo Video, Albuquerque, NM. Assisted in production of cable television shows, documentaries, and special events; duties included camera work, editing, research, and administrative support

Summer 1992   **Associate Computer-Games Specialist.** Lucasdigital Ltd., Lucusfilm Ltd., Lucasarts Entertainment Co., San Raphael, CA. Assisted game developers and artists in developing computer software games; utilized 2-D computer graphic art/animation techniques in producing computer games

EDUCATION

1992   **Professional Diploma in Film Production,** Honors, University of
Wisconsin-Madison, Madison, WI
     Coursework:
- Film Styles and Genres
- Critical Film Analysis
- The American Film Industry in the Age of Television
- Video Production and Direction
- Advanced Motion Picture Production
- Film Colloquium
- Seminar Radio, Television, Film
- Seminar in Film Theory

     Recipient:
- The Mary Elizabeth Tucker-Chaffin Fellowship

1990   **Master of Fine Arts,** High Honors, West Virginia University,
Morgantown, WV
     Major: Acting
     Coursework:
- Directed Theatre Studies
- Advanced Technical Theatre
- Costume History
- Creative Dramatics
- Puppetry
- Advanced Playwriting
- Classic Theatre
- Advanced Graduate Vocal Techniques
- Movement
- Advanced Graduate Stage Movement
- Graduate Acting Studio
- Period Style
- Graduate Colloquium

     Recipient:
- W. E. B. DuBois Fellowship; the Anthony Wayne Tucker Fellowship

MOIRA ELSPETH SOAMES
page three

1987   **Bachelor of Fine Arts,** cum laude, Fashion Institute of Fine Arts, New
York, NY
Major: toy design Minor: dance

SCHOLARSHIPS

1991   **Presidential Scholar in the Arts Award,** Presidential Scholar in the
Arts Recognition and Talent Search. Awarded by the National Foundation
for Advancement in the Arts (NFAA). Honored at the White House and
received $1000

1993   **National Ten-Minute Play Contest,** Actors Theatre of Louisville,
Louisville, KY
One-act play *Love Au Gratin*

AFFILIATIONS

American Film Institute
Association of Visual Communicators
Toy Manufacturers of America
USITT: The American Association of Design and Production Professionals in
the Performing Arts

MENZIES H. QING

3401 Assylum Avenue
Hartford, CT 06705

203 768-1900
E-mail: Menzies@aol.hartford.com

Keywords

Television. Theology. Religion. Philosophy. Culture. Chinese. PhD Harvard University. MDiv Graduate Theological Union. BA University of Melbourne, Australia. WPIX-TV Channel 11. WIHN-TV. WTNH-TV Channel 8. CBS "60 Minutes." Talk Show Host. Copy Editor. Researcher. Interviewer. Charlie Rose. Oprah Winfrey. Mike Wallace. Sally Jesse Raphael. Windows 2000. Communication Skills. Accurate. Adaptable. Aggressive. Analytical. Conceptual. Articulate. Creative. Public Speaking. High Energy. Persuasive. Tenacious.

Professional Objective

A position hosting television programs that present discourse on philosophical, theological, and religious perspectives of cultures in America.

Education

1995   PhD, **THE UNIVERSITY OF MICHIGAN,** Ann Arbor, MI
Major: Systematic and Philosophical Theology and Philosophy of Religion
Dissertation: "Theological and Philosophical Perspectives of God and Man in the Writings of Paul Tillich and Pierre Teilhard de Chardin" Coursework:
- Themes in African American Religious History
- Current Trends in American Judaism
- Aramaic/Rabbinic Hebrew
- Hermeneutics and Christian Theories: An Historical Survey
- Theories of Religion and Culture
- Medieval Religious Texts
- World Religions
- Otherness and History in the Study of Religion
- Seminar in Systematic Philosophy
- Advanced Problems in Philosophy of Language
- Observation and Interpretation of Religious Action
- Seminar in Philosophical Theology
- Islam

MENZIES H. QING 2

1990   MDiv, **GRADUATE THEOLOGICAL UNION,** Berkeley, CA
  Major: Cultural and Historical Study of Religion
  Thesis: "History of Religion in America: 1980–1990"
  Coursework:
- Religion, Fundamentalism, and Nationalism
- Modern Western Religious Thought
- Religion and Anthropology
- History of Religion in America Since 1865
- Ethnicity, Race, and Religion in America
- Public Religion in US History
- Sufism
- Topics in Comparative Religions
- Buddhism
- Understanding World Religions in Multicultural Contexts

1987   BA, **UNIVERSITY OF MELBOURNE,** Melbourne, Australia
  Major: Asian Languages and Literatures
  Specialty: Chinese Language and Literatures

Awards

January 1995   **Beinecke Library Short-Term Fellowship,** Yale University
Researched publications in medieval philosophy in the Beinecke Rare Book and Manuscript Library

1984   **Sidney E. Mead Prize.** Awarded for best essay—"History of Religion in America: 1960–1970"—in the field of church history by a doctoral candidate

Experience

1995   **Researcher,** "The Charlie Rose Show," II WCNY-TV, New York, NY. Reviewed publications and prepared program notes

Summer 1994   **Copy Editor,** "60 Minutes," CBS TELEVISION. Prepared information for Mike Wallace's program segments

1994   **Interviewer/Prompter,** "The Oprah Winfrey Show," CBS TELEVISION. Interviewed show guests

Summer 1993   **Interviewer/Prompter,** "Sally Jesse Raphael," STUDIOS USA. Interviewed show guests

MENZIES H. QING 3

Summer 1993	**Newscaster,** WPIX-TV Channel 11, New York, NY. Weekend news co-anchor.
1989–1991	**Intern/Panelist,** AUSTRALIAN BROADCASTING COMPANY, New York, NY. Panelist on programs describing American culture for broadcast in Australia; edited scripts for guests
Summer 1988	**Model,** THE de l'Orme AGENCY, Boston, MA. Appeared on television in automobile commercials

Skills

Language: Conversationally fluent in Chinese
Proficient in French

Computer: Software and programming in C, C++, and visual BASIC in Windows NT and WNIX environments

Interests

Chinese language and theatre; Dead Sea Scrolls; theology; sailing; swimming; television

Checklist for Preparing Scannable Curricula Vitae[2]

_____ Select keywords carefully and arrange them in an order that complements the categories of your CV. They should not only appear in the KEYWORD category but also in other parts of your CV. (Consult *The Electronic Resume Revolution* for guidance in using keywords.)

_____ Use a popular, common typeface such as Times New Roman, Tahoma, or Arial.

_____ Use a font size between 12 and 14 points. Your name, however, should always appear in a font at the upper end of this range.

_____ Avoid italics, script, and underlined passages.

_____ Do not use graphics and shading.

_____ Use horizontal and vertical lines sparingly. If you use them, however, allow a quarter-inch of white space around them.

_____ Use a laser or DeskJet printer.

_____ Use 8½ × 11 inch white paper.

_____ Place your name at the very top of the first page and all subsequent pages of your CV. It must be on a line by itself.

_____ Avoid stapling or folding your CV.

_____ Use boldface and/or all capital letters as long as the letters do not touch each other.

_____ Avoid two-column formats.

_____ Use standard address format below your name.

_____ List each telephone number on its own line.

_____ Do not condense spacing between letters.

---

[2]Adapted from Kennedy and Morrow. *The Electronic Resume Revolution,* 2nd ed. New York: John Wiley & Sons, 1995.

In addition to scannable curriculum vitae, prospective employers also accept E-mailed and online CVs, as well as those submitted to CV banks. As a general rule, however, they do not search for home page CVs. Prospective employers prefer E-mailed curricula vitae because there are far fewer formatting errors for them to correct. Remember to include a cover letter and to place your E-mail address and telephone number on all pages. Before E-mailing your CV, find out whether prospective employers prefer to receive CVs as attachments or as part of the E-mail itself.[3]

---

[3]West, Linda. "E-Mail Resumes—The New Trend in Recruitment." 2002. *ProvenResumes.com.* 14 April 2002. www.provenresumes.com/reswkshps/electronic/emlres.html

International Curricula Vitae

For bilingual and international applicants, we have included sample curricula vitae written in French, German, and Spanish. With regard to content, organization, and format, please note that similar principles discussed in previous chapters often apply to the creation of CVs written in languages other than English. However, there are some differences. For example, French CVs always include the applicant's passport photograph; passport photos on German CVs are optional. You can learn about cultural differences in creating curricula vitae by consulting your professors, advisors, or mentors.

We are especially grateful to Dr. Orlando Reyes-Cairo, who wrote the Spanish language CV.

L E B E N S L A U F

Rainer Müller

PERSÖNLICHE DATEN

geb. am: 25. Juni 1971

Geburtsort: Kirrberg/Saarland

Wohnhaft in: Weinbrennerstraße 11
                    Saarbrücken
                    D-6600

Familienstand: ledig

Staatsangehörigkeit: deutsch

SCHULAUSBILDUNG

1981–1991   Gymnasium Johanneum
                    Abitur

WEHRDIENST

1991–1993   15 Monate Grundwehrdienst
                    (Marine)

STUDIUM

                    Studiumaufnahme an der Universität des Saarlandes in den Hauptfächern
                    Germanistik und Anglistik und in dem Nebenfach Amerikanistik

1994–1996   DAAD-Stipendiat am Ohio University in Athens, Ohio, USA

1996–1997   1. Staatsarbeit: ,,Water Imagery in James Joyce's *Ulysses*"
                    1. Staatsexamen: Note, sehr gut

2000   2. Staatsarbeit: ,,The Grotesque in Flannery O'Connor's *Wise Blood* and
                                    Selected Short Stories"
                    2. Staatsexamen: Note, sehr gut

2000–2002   Referendariat am Gymnasium am Krebsberg in Neunkirchen/Saarland

SPRACHKENNTNISSE

Deutsch: Muttersprache
Englisch: sehr gut
Französisch: Grundkenntnisse

André Michel[1]
Né le 08/02/70
560, Rue de la Révolution
95110 SANNOIS
France

Téléphone: 4.96.38.82.61
E-mail: andré.michel@laposte.net

```
place
photo
here
```

Éducation

février 1997	*Maîtrise d'Informatique et Mathématique* Université de Nantes
juin 1993	*Licence d'Informatiques* Université de Nantes

Expériences professionnelles

depuis novembre 2000	Développement avec FoxPro 2.6 d'un logiciel pour l'industrie du vêtement; installation et support de systèmes PC, basés sur DOS, Windows 2000 et Windows NT FoxSoftware Saint-Hubert, Québec
septembre 1999 à novembre 2000	SSII Eurotechnologie Administration Système sous Novell et Windows NT; développement et extension de logiciel sur PC pour des applications C, Basic et Pascal Paris, France

Expériences professionnelles, suite

juin 1998 à octobre 2000	Stage, développeur C sous Unix, société 35 GlobalNet Paris, France
juin 1997 à juin 1998	Ingénieur de développement, société Encrease Cologne, Zurich, Frankfurt

---

[1]The following websites were consulted to prepare this CV:
www.amath.net/perso/MarcGuillemot.htm
www.ressources-web.com/cv/informatique/BOUCHARD.htm
www.ressources-web.com/cv/informatique/CV%20(2).htm
www.ressources-web.com/cv/informatique/BEBERIDE.htm

André Michel

Connaissances..

Langages de programmations:

- COBOL
- Scheme
- C
- C++

- Pascal
- ColdFusion
- Delphi
- XML

- VisualBasic
- JAVA
- php
- JavaScript

Langages de développement Web:

- JavaServer
- Page
- HTML
- JavaScript
- BroadVision 4 et 5

Autres:

- Windows 2000
- NT Serveur
- Hyena
- Insight Manager

Aptitudes..

Administration, installation et paramètrage de serveurs:

- Novell 5.1
- NT 2000

- Windows NT
- Compaq

Langues:

- français: langue maternelle
- anglais: courant
- allemand: courant

Divers...

- cèlibataire
- mobilité géographique internationale
- sport: football
- musique

Ce curriculum vitae est dispinible en allemenad sur demande.

Fait le 06/08/02

CURRICULULUM VITAE

ORLANDO M. REYES-CAIRO
Owens Community College
P.O. Box 10,000, Toledo, Ohio 43699-1947
Teléfono: (419) 661-7935
Correo electrónico: oreyes-cairo@owens.edu

DATOS PERSONALES

Nacido y criado en Cuba. Actualmente ciudadano norteamericano naturalizado.

EDUCACIÓN

PRE-UNIVERSITARIA

Escuela Primaria Don Tomás Estrada Palma, Jagüey Grande, Matanzas, Cuba.

Escuela Superior Félix Varela, Jagüey Grande, Matanzas, Cuba.

Escuela Presbiteriana *La Progresiva,* Cárdenas, Matanzas, Cuba. Bachillerato.

UNIVERSITARIA

Licenciatura en Filosofía y Letras—Universidad de Dakota del Sur, Vermillion,   1958
Dakota del Sur.

      Campo de Concentracíon: Lengua y Literatura Española

      Campos Secundarios: Ciencia Aplicada, Francés, Teatro

Master en Letra—Universidad de Minnesota, Minneapolis, Minnesota.   1962

      Campo de Concentracíon: Literatura Española

      Campos Secundarios: Francés y Teatro

Doctorado en Filosofía—Lingüística Románica. Universidad de Michigan,   1970
Ann Arbor, Michigan.

      Tesis Doctoral: "Utterance—Final Frequency and Amplitude Contours
         in the Perception of Questions in Spanish"

PREMIOS Y HONORES

National Defense Foreign Language Fellowship. Universidad de Michigan,   1962–1964
Ann Arbor.

Rackham Dissertation Fellowship. Escuela de Estudios Graduados Rackham,
Universidad de Michigan, Ann Arbor. 1968–1969

Profesor Emérito. Universidad de Toledo, Toledo, Ohio. 1989

Curriculum Vitae: Orlando M. Reyes-Cairo 2

EXPERIENCIA

DOCENTE

Candler College, Marianao, Habana, Cuba. Inglés.	1956–1957
Escuela Metodista Central, Habana, Cuba. Inglés.	1956–1957
Universidad de Minnesota, Minneápolis, Minnesota. Español.	1960–1962
Universidad de Tecnología Lamar, Beaumont, Tejas. Español.	1964–1965
Universidad de Purdue, West Lafayette, Indiana. Español y Lingüística.	1965–1968
Curso intensivo de español para el Programa de Asistencia en la América Latina de la Universidad de Purdue.	Verano de 1966
Universidad de Toledo, Toledo, Ohio. Español y Lingüística.	1969–1989
Cuatro cursos especiales sobre cultura hispánica para el Centro de Entrenamiento y Educación de Justicia Criminal en Toledo, Ohio.	1983
Colegio Universitario Comunitario Owens, Toledo, Ohio. Español.	1999–presente

ACTIVIDADES PROFESIONALES EN LA UNIVERSIDAD DE TOLEDO

CURSOS CREADOS EN LA UNIVERSIDAD DE TOLEDO

Español para chicanos
Sintaxis y estilística
Lingüística románica
Literatura infantil española
Historia de la lengua española
Teatro español práctico
La estructura del español moderno
Seminario de lingüística española
Pronunciación de lenguas modernas: alemán, español, francés e italiano
Introducción a la lingüística
Español comercial
Cultura hispánica

MATERIALES CREADOS

Materiales para cursos de conversación en español
Texto para el curso de Sintaxis y estilística
Monografía para texto de Cultura hispánica

Curriculum Vitae: Orlando M. Reyes-Cairo   3

PROGRAMAS CREADOS

Programa de Verano en México (con colaboración)

Colaboración en la creación del Programa Lingüístico

Programa de Estudios Chicanos (con colaboración)

Programa de Intercambio Estudiantil con la Universidad de Toledo, España
(con colaboración)

Programa Intensivo de Capacitación en Español para la División de Educación
de Adultos

Programa de Lenguas Críticas

DIRECCIÓN DE PROGRAMAS

Codirector del Programa de Verano en México	1972
Director del Programa de Verano en México	1973–1975
Director del Programa de Lenguas Críticas	1975–1977

PARTICIPACIÓN EN COMITÉS

Miembro de 13 comités del Departamento de Lenguas Extranjeras, en cinco
como presidente Participación en 3 comités de la facultad de Artes y Ciencias

PARTICIPACIÓN EN OTRAS ACTIVIDADES ACADÉMICAS

Secretario de la Sociedad Honoraria Sigma Delta Pi	1973–1976
Consejero de Estudiantes Graduados	1975–1987

ACTIVIDADES PROFESIONALES EN EL COLEGIO UNIVERSITARIO OWENS

CURSO CREADO

Cultura Hispánica

PARTICIPACIÓN EN COMITÉS

Varios comités departamentales

Comité Universitario sobre Culturas Mundiales

Concilio de Planeamiento Universitario

Comité de Evaluación de Rango

EXPERIENCIA RELACIONADA CON LA DOCENCIA

PARTICIPACIÓN EN REUNIONES PROFESIONALES

Asistencia a la Conferencia Bicultural-Bilingüe auspiciada por el Centro
para el Desarrollo de la Educación y los Servicios Estratégicos de
Kent Estatal en Toledo   Febrero de 1975

Curriculum Vitae: Orlando M. Reyes-Cairo   4

Asistencia a la Conferencia de la Asociación Nacional para los
     Programas de Lenguas Auto-Instruccionales (NASILP), en
     Buffalo, N.Y., en preparación para asumir la responsabilidad
     de Director del Programa de Lenguas Críticas   1975

Asistencia a la Conferencia sobre Carreras Bilingües en Comercio en
     la Universidad del Este de Michigan   Marzo de 1982

Moderador de la Sesión sobre Variaciones Dialectales en América
     durante la Conferencia sobre la Política de Lenguas en América
     en la Universidad de Toledo   Abril de 1982

Asistencia a la Conferencia del Sistema de Información Nacional del
     Departamento de Educación de Ohio en el Centro de Desarrollo
     y Entrenamiento del Colegio Universitario Owens   Mayo de 2000

Participación en la Conferencia Cumbre IV de Inglés para Hablantes de
     Otras Lenguas (ESOL) en Columbus, Ohio   Mayo de 2000

Asistencia a la Conferencia de Maestros de Inglés para Hablantes de
     Otras Lenguas (TESOL) y (LAU) en Columbus, Ohio   Octubre de 2000

Participacíon en la Conferencia Cumbre V de Ingles para Hablantes
     de Otras Lenguas (ESOL) en Columbus, Ohio   Diciembre de 2000

Miembro del Grupo de Creación de Normas para el Contenido
     Académico de Lenguas Extranjeras creado por el Departamento
     de Educación del Estado de Ohio   2002–presente

PONENCIAS EN REUNIONES PROFESIONALES

Enfoques modernos a los estudios de lenguas modernas. Seminario sobre
     Lenguas Extranjeras en la escuela secundaria Start, patrocinado
     por el Consejo de Educación de Toledo.   Octubre de 1969

A Final Word

We encourage you to use the information presented in this book to prepare your curriculum vitae and accompanying correspondence, as well as to remember and continue throughout your life the creative reflection that produced it. Our hortatory tone notwithstanding, we trust you will use this experience in producing your CV as a springboard for continued reflection on who you are and what you want to accomplish in the future.

Discerning readers of *How to Prepare Your Curriculum Vitae* will recall that the CV, as least as it has often been constructed and disseminated in academic circles, has always been viewed as an extension of notions of academic freedom. From this perspective, it has been shielded from any trend toward standardization or orthodoxy, which has become the fate of the traditional résumé.

Members of the academy have always insisted on describing their academic and work backgrounds without regard for any commonly agreed upon standards except those promulgated by professional associations and learned and scientific societies. This practice has often resulted in CVs of unusual length and confusing organization.

Not surprisingly, some movement toward changing this situation has occurred. *How to Prepare Your Curriculum Vitae* is a significant part of this change. It emphasizes adherence to writing styles and documentation guidelines of professional associations and learned or scientific societies; at the same time, it encourages the use of document design guidelines that enhance the overall presentation of the CV. These changes have been largely occasioned by the increasing use of CVs outside the academy. Moreover, technological advancements such as the Internet, electronic record keeping, data storage, and informational transmission have also contributed to changes in the content, format, design, and dissemination of CVs.

Our text has taken you beyond typical publications that simply end by saying "the process of preparing your CV is complete; you are now on your own." We are, rather, suggesting that you reflect on the skills you have acquired as a result of completing your degree(s) as well as on the skills you have honed as a result of preparing your CV. Furthermore, we urge you to use these skills in your professional development, career planning, and life-long learning.

We trust that the preparation of your CV and accompanying correspondence has been, and will continue to be, a rewarding experience. We wish you only success.

Appendix A: Action Verbs

accelerated
accommodated
accomplished
accounted for
achieved
acquainted
acquired
activated
adapted
added
adjusted
administered
advertised
advised
advocated
aided
alphabetized
altered
analyzed

anticipated
applied
appointed
appraised
approved
arbitrated
argued
arranged
assembled
assessed
assisted
assumed
attached
attained
attended
augmented
authored
authorized
balanced

bolstered
boosted
briefed
budgeted
built
calculated
catalogued
caused
chaired
changed
checked
classified
cleared up
collected
combined
commanded
communicated
compared
completed

composed
conceived
concluded
condensed
conditioned
conducted
conferred
consolidated
constructed
consulted
contracted
controlled
converted
convinced
coordinated
copied
corrected
counseled
counted

crafted
created
critiqued
curtailed
debated
decided
defined
delegated
delivered
demonstrated
designated
designed
determined
developed
devised
diminished
directed
disclosed
discontinued
discovered
dispatched
displayed
distributed
drafted
dramatized
earned
economized
edited
educated
elected
eliminated
employed
encouraged
endorsed
enlarged
enlisted
ensured
entered
established
estimated
evaluated
examined
excelled
exchanged
executed
exercised
exhibited
expanded
expedited
explained
explored
extended

familiarized
filed
financed
forecast
foresaw
formulated
fostered
found
gathered
governed
graded
greeted
grossed
grouped
guaranteed
guided
handled
hastened
heightened
helped
highlighted
identified
illustrated
implemented
improved
included
incorporated
increased
informed
initiated
inspected
instructed
interpreted
interviewed
introduced
inventoried
invested
investigated
joined
judged
labored
launched
lectured
led
located
maintained
managed
mapped out
maximized
measured
merged
minimized

modernized
modified
monitored
motivated
negotiated
notified
observed
obtained
opened
operated
ordered
organized
originated
overcame
oversaw
paid
painted
participated
perceived
performed
persuaded
pioneered
planned
policed
prepared
prescribed
presented
prevailed
processed
procured
produced
profited
programmed
prohibited
projected
promoted
proofed
proved
publicized
published
purchased
qualified
rated
received
recognized
recommended
rectified
reduced
regulated
related
removed
renovated

reorganized
repaired
replaced
reported
rescued
researched
restored
resulted in
returned
revealed
reviewed
revised
saved
screened
scrutinized
selected
sent
served
set
shipped
showed
sifted
simplified
smoothed
solved
sought
spearheaded
specified
spoke
sponsored
stabilized
started
stopped
straightened
streamlined
strengthened
stripped
studied
submitted
suggested
supervised
supplemented
surpassed
taught
terminated
trained
transferred
transformed
unified
updated
utilized
vetoed

Appendix B: Selected United States and Canadian Professional, Learned, and Scientific Societies

The U.S. listings in this appendix appear in *National Trade and Professional Associations of the United States* (Washington, DC: Columbia Books, Inc., 2001). The Canadian listings are from *Corpus Almanac and Canadian Sourcebook* (Third annual ed. Don Mills, Ontario: Southam, Inc., 1997).

United States

Anthropology

American Anthropological Association
4350 North Fairfax Drive, Suite 640
Arlington, VA 22202
Tel: (703) 528-1903
Fax: (703) 528-3546
Internet: www.aaanet.org

Archaeology

Archaeological Institute of America
Boston University
656 Beacon Street, Fourth Floor
Boston, MA 02215-2006
Tel: (617) 353-9361
Fax: (617) 353-6550
E-mail: aia@aia.bu.edu
Internet: www.archaeological.org

Architecture

American Institute of Architects
1735 New York Avenue NW
Washington, DC 02215-5292
Tel: (202) 626-7300
Fax: (202) 626-7426
Internet: www.aia.org

Arts

American Council for the Arts
1 East Fifty-Third Street
New York, NY 10022
Tel: (212) 233-2787
Fax: (212) 980-4857
Internet: www.artsusa.org

Biology

American Institute of Biological Sciences
730 Eleventh Street NW
Washington, DC 20001-4521
Tel: (202) 628-1500
Fax: (202) 628-1509
E-mail: admin@aibs.org
Internet: www.aibs.org

Chemistry

American Chemical Society
1155 Sixteenth Street NW
Washington, DC 20036
Tel: (202) 872-4600
Fax: (202) 872-4615

Computer Science

Computing Research Association
1100 Seventeenth Street NW, Suite 507
Washington, DC 20036-4632
Tel: (202) 234-2111
Fax: (202) 667-1066
E-mail: info@cra.org
Internet: http://cra.org

Dentistry	American Dental Association 211 East Chicago Avenue Chicago, IL 60611-2678 Tel: (312) 440-2500 Fax: (312) 440-2800 Internet: www.ada.org
Economics	American Economic Association 2014 Broadway, Suite 305 Nashville, TN 37203-2418 Tel: (615) 322-2595 Fax: (615) 343-7590 E-mail: aeainfo@ctrvax.vanderbilt.edu
Engineering	National Society of Professional Engineers 1420 King Street Alexandria, VA 22314-2794 Tel: (703) 684-2800 Internet: www.nspe.org
Geography	American Geographical Society 4220 King Street Alexandria, VA 22303 Tel: (703) 379-2480 Fax: (703) 379-7563
Geology	American Geophysical Union 2000 Florida Avenue NW Washington, DC 20009-1277 Tel: (202) 462-6900; (800) 966-2481 Fax: (202) 328-0566 Internet: www.agu.org
History	American Historical Association 400 A Street SE Washington, DC 20003-3889 Tel: (202) 544-2422 Fax: (202) 544-8307 E-mail: aha@theahe.org
Language	Modern Language Association of America 10 Astor Place New York, NY 10003-6981 Tel: (212) 475-9500 Fax: (212) 477-9863 Internet: www.mla.org
Law	American Bar Association 750 North Lake Shore Drive Chicago, IL 60611-6281 Tel: (312) 988-5000 Fax: (312) 988-6281 Internet: www.abanet.org

Linguistics   Linguistics Society of America
1325 Eighteenth Street NW, Suite 211
Washington, DC 20036-6501
Tel: (202) 835-1714
Fax: (202) 835-1717
E-mail: lsa@lsadc.org
Internet: www.lsadc.org

Mathematics   Mathematical Association of America
1529 Eighteenth Street NW
Washington, DC 20036
Tel: (202) 387-5200
Fax: (202) 379-7563
Internet: www.maa.org

Medicine   American Medical Association
515 North State Street
Chicago, IL 60610
Tel: (312) 464-4814; (800) 621-8335
Fax: (312) 464-4184
Internet: www.ama-assn.org

Music   American Society of Music Arrangers and Composers
P.O. Box 11
Hollywood, CA 90078
Tel: (213) 658-5997
E-mail: info@asmac.org
Internet: www.asmac.org

International Association of Jazz Educators
P.O. Box 724
Manhattan, KS 66502
Tel: (785) 776-8744
Fax: (785) 776-6190

Philosophy   American Philosophical Society
104 South Fifth Street
Philadelphia, PA 19106-3387
Tel: (213) 440-3434
Fax: (215) 440-3436
Internet: www.amphilsoc.org

Physics   American Institute of Physics
1 Physics Ellipse
College Park, MD 20740-3843
Tel: (301) 209-3100
Fax: (301) 209-0840
E-mail: aipinfo@aip.org

Political Science   American Political Science Association
1527 New Hampshire Avenue NW
Washington, DC 20036
Tel: (202) 483-2512
Fax: (202) 483-2657

Psychology   American Psychological Association
750 First Street NE
Washington, DC 20002-4242
Tel: (202) 336-5510; (800) 374-2721
Fax: (202) 336-5708
Internet: www.apa.org

Religion   American Academy of Religion
1703 Clifton Road NE, Suite G-5
Atlanta, GA 30329-4019
Tel: (404) 727-7920
Fax: (404) 727-7959
Internet: www.aarweb.org/Default.asp

Sociology   American Sociological Association
1307 New York Avenue NW, Suite 700
Washington, DC 20005
Tel: (202) 383-9005
Internet: www.asanet.org

Theater   American Society for Theatre Research
Department of Theatre, Fine Arts
University of Rhode Island
Kingston, RI 02881-0824
Tel: (401) 874-5921
Fax: (401) 874-5618

Dramatists Guild of America, Inc.
1501 Broadway, Suite 701
New York, NY 10036
Tel: (212) 398-9366
Fax: (212) 944-0420
Internet: www.dramaguild.com

Canada

Architecture   The Royal Architecture Institute of Canada
55 Murray Street, Suite 330
Ottawa, ON K1N 5M3
Tel: (613) 241-3600
Fax: (613) 241-5750

Society for the Study of Architecture in Canada
Box 2302, Suite D
Ottawa, ON K1P 5W5
Tel: (416) 961-9956
Fax: (416) 585-2389

Arts   Canadian Conference of the Arts/Conférence canadienne des arts
c/o Keith Kelly, National Director
189 Laurier Avenue E
Ottawa, ON K1N 6P1
Tel: (613) 238-3561
Fax: (613) 238-4849
E-mail: ccart@globalx.net

Conseil de la peinture du Québec
911, rue Jean-Talon Est. Bur. 120
Montréal, QC H2R 1V5
Tel: (514) 279-5600

Royal Canadian Academy of Arts
163 Queen Street E, Box 2
Toronto, ON M5A 1S1
Tel: (416) 408-2718
Fax: (416) 363-9612

Biology

Canadian Federation of Biological Societies, Inc. (CFBS)/Fédération
canadienne des sociétes de biologie, inc.
104-1750 Courtwood Crescent
Ottawa, ON K2C 2B5
Tel: (613) 225-8889
Fax: (613) 224-9621
E-mail: cfbS@hpb.hwc.ca

Chemistry

The Chemical Institute of Canada
130 Slater Street, Suite 550
Ottawa, ON K1P 6E2
Tel: (613) 232-6252
Fax: (613) 232-5862
E-mail: cic_adm@FoxNSTY.CA
Internet: www.chem-inst-can.org

Cinema and Film

Academy of Canadian Cinema and Television/Academie canadienne du
cinema et de la télévision
158 Pearl Street
Toronto, ON M5H 1L3
Tel: (416) 591-2040
Fax: (416) 591-2157
Internet: www.academy.ca

Orde des architects du Québec
1825 boulevard René-Lévesque Quest
Montréal, QC H3H 1R4
Tel: (514) 937-6168; (800) 599-6168
Fax: (514) 933-0242

Canadian Film Institute/Institut canadienne du film
2 Daly Avenue
Ottawa, ON K1N 6E2
Tel: (613) 232-6727
Fax: (613) 232-6315
E-mail: cv534@freenet.carlton.ca

Computer and
Information Processing

Association of Professional Computer Consultants
2175 Sheppard Avenue E, Suite 310
Willowdale, ON M2J 1W8
Tel: (416) 491-3556
Fax: (416) 491-1670

Canadian Association for Information Science
University of Toronto
140 St. George Street
Toronto, ON M5S 3G6
Tel: (416) 978-8876
Fax: (416) 971-1399

Canadian Information Processing Society
430 King Street W, Suite 106
Toronto, ON M5V 1L5
Tel: (416) 593-4040
Fax: (416) 593-5184
E-mail: infor@cips.ca

Information Technology Association of Canada (ITAC), Inc.
2800 Skymark Avenue, Suite 402
Mississaugua, ON L4W 5A6
Tel: (905) 602-8346
Fax: (905) 602-8346
E-mail: infor@itac.ca

Dentistry   Canadian Dental Association
1815 Alta Vista Drive
Ottawa, ON K1G 3Y6
Tel: (613) 523-1770
Fax: (613) 523-7736

Economics   Canadian Economics Association
University of Toronto
Department of Economics
150 St. George Street
Toronto, ON M5S 3G7
Tel: (416) 978-6295
Fax: (416) 978-6713
E-mail: denny@epas.ntoronto.ca

Engineering   Canadian Association for Composite Structures and Materials
(CACSMA)/Association canadienne pour les structures et materiaux
composites
Sylvie Lamontagne, Administrative Secretary
75 boulevard De Montagne
Boucherville, QC J4B 6Y4
Tel: (514) 641-5139
Fax: (514) 641-5117

Association des Diplömés de Polytechnique
Lucille Charbonneau, directrice d'admin.
C.P. 6079, succ. Centre-Ville
Montréal, QC H3C 3A7
Tel: (514) 340-4764
Fax: (514) 340-4472

Association of Consulting Engineers of Canada/Association des
ingenieurs-conseils du Canada
Pierre A. H. Franche, President/CEO
130 Albert Street, Suite 616
Ottawa, ON K1P 5G4
Tel: (613) 236-0569
Fax: (613) 236-6193
E-mail: exec@asec.ca

Geography   Canadian Association of Geographers/L'Association canadienne
des geographes
Burnside Hall
McGill University
805 rue Sherbrooke ouest
Montréal, QC H3A 2K6
Tel: (514) 398-4946
Fax: (514) 398-7437
E-mail: cag@felix.georg.mcgill.ca

Royal Canadian Geographical Society
39 McArthur Avenue
Vanier, ON K1L 8L7
Tel: (613) 745-4629
Fax: (613) 744-0947

Geology   Geological Association of Canada
Department of Earth Sciences
Memorial University of Newfoundland
St John's, NF A1B 3X5
Tel: (709) 737-7660
Fax: (709) 737-2532
E-mail: gag@sparky2.esd.mun.ca
Internet: www.esd.mun.ca/~gac

History   Canadian Historical Association/Société historique du Canada
395 Wellington Street
Ottawa, ON K1A 0N3
Tel: (613) 233-7885
Fax: (613) 567-3110
E-mail: jmineault@archives.ca

Law   Canadian Bar Association/L'Association du Barreau canadien
55 O'Connor Street, Suite 902
Ottawa, ON K1P 6L2
Tel: (613) 237-2925
Fax: (613) 237-0185

Linguistics   Canadian Linguistic Association, Inc./L'Association canadienne de
liguistique inc.
Memorial University
St. John's, NG A1C 5S8
Tel: (709) 737-8255
Fax: (709) 737-2135

Mathematics   Canadian Mathematical Society, Inc./L'Association candienne de
linguistique inc.
577 King Edward Avenue, Suite 109
Ottawa, ON K1N 6N5
Tel: (613) 562-5702
Fax: (613) 565-1539

Medicine   Association of Canadian Medical Colleges
774 Echo Drive
Ottawa, ON K1S 5P2
Tel: (613) 730-0687
Fax: (613) 730-1196
E-mail: acmd@rcpsc.edu

The Royal College of Physicians and Surgeons of Canada
774 Echo Drive
Ottawa, ON K1S 5N8
Tel: (613) 730-6201
Fax: (613) 730-2410
E-mail: pierrettee.leonard@rcosc.edu

Music   Black Music Association of Canada
59 Chester Hill Road
Toronto, ON M4K 1X4
Tel: (416) 463-8880
Fax: (416) 463-8880

Canadian League of Composers
20 St. Joseph Street
Toronto, ON M4Y 1J9
Tel: (416) 964-1364

Physics   Canadian Association of Physicists/Association canadienne des
physiciens et physiciennes
MacDonald Building
150 Louis Pasteur, Suite 112
Ottawa, ON K1N 6N5
Tel: (613) 562-5614
Fax: (613) 562-5615

Political Science   Canadian Political Science Association
1 Stewart Street, Suite 205
Ottawa, ON K1N 6H7
Tel: (613) 564-4026
Fax: (613) 230-274

Sociology and Anthropology   Canadian Sociology and Anthropology Association
Concordia University
1445, boulevard de Maisouneuve ouest
bur. LB-615
Montréal, QC H3G 1M8
Tel: (514) 848-8780
Fax: (514) 848-4539

Appendix C: Suggested Reading

Selected Stylebooks and Manuals

American Society of Journalists & Authors Staff. *Tools of the Trade: Successful Writers Tell All About the Equipment & Services They Find the Best.* New York: HarperCollins, 1990.

American Psychological Association. *Publication Manual of the American Psychological Association.* 4th ed. Washington, DC: American Psychological Association, 2001.

Brown, Bill Wesley. *Successful Technical Writing.* South Holland, IL: The Goodheart-Wilcox Co., Inc., 2000.

The CBE Manual for Authors and Publishers. Scientific Style and Format. 6th ed. Cambridge, MA: Cambridge University, 1999.

Crewes, Frederick. *The Random House Handbook.* New York: McGraw-Hill, Inc., 1992.

DeBries, Mary A. *Prentice Hall Style Manual.* Englewood Cliffs, NJ: Prentice Hall, 1992.

Dodd, Janet S., and Marianne C. Brogan. *The ACS Style Guide: A Manual for Authors and Editors.* Washington, DC: American Chemical Society, 1997.

Dumond, Val. *The Elements of Nonsexist Usage.* New York: Prentice Hall Press, 1990.

Fowler, H. Ramsey, and Jane E. Aaron. *The Little Brown Handbook.* New York: HarperCollins, 2002.

Jordan, Lewis. *The New York Times Manual of Style and Usage.* New York: Quadrangle New York Times Book Co., 1999.

Karls, John B., and Ronald Szymanski. *The Writer's Handbook.* Lincolnwood, IL: National Textbook Co., 1994.

Kirszner, Laurie G., and Stephen R. Mandell. *Holt Handbook.* 3rd ed. New York: Harcourt Brace, 2002.

Lerner, Marcia. *Writing Smart: Your Guide to Great Writing.* New York: Random House, 2001.

Longyear, Marie. *The McGraw-Hill Style Manual.* New York: McGraw-Hill, 1989.

Luey, Beth. *Handbook for Academic Authors.* rev. ed. Cambridge, MA: Cambridge University Press, 2002.

Lynch, Patrick J. *Web Style Guide: Basic Principles for Creating Web Sites.* New Haven, CT: Yale University Press, 1997.

Marins, Richard. *A Writer's Companion.* 3rd ed. New York: McGraw-Hill, 1997.

New York Public Library. *Writer's Guide to Style and Usage.* New York: HarperCollins, 1994.

Nickerson, Marie-Louise. *The Scribner Workbook for Writers.* Boston, MA: Allyn and Bacon, 1995.

Rubens, Philip, ed. *Science and Technical Writing. A Manual of Style.* New York: Henry Holt, 2000.

Shelton, James H. *Handbook for Technical Writing.* Lincolnwood, IL: NTC Business Books, 1999.

Steinmann, Manin, and Michael Keller. *NTC's Handbook for Writers.* Lincolnwood, IL: NTC Publishing Group, 1995.

Strunk, William, Jr., and E.B. White. *The Elements of Style.* 3rd ed. New York: Macmillan Publishing Co., 1979.

Turabian, Kate L. *A Manual for Writers of Term Papers, Theses, and Dissertations.* 6th ed. Chicago, IL: University of Chicago Press, 1996.

United Press International. *The UPI Stylebook.* 3rd ed. Lincolnwood, IL: National Textbook Co., 1995.

The University of Chicago Press. *The Chicago Manual of Style: The Essential Guide for Writers, Editors, and Publishers.* 14th ed. Chicago, IL: University of Chicago Press, 1993.

Williams, Joseph M. *Style: Toward Clarity and Grace.* Chicago, IL: University of Chicago Press, 1995.

Zacharias, Johanna. *A Style Guide for CBO.* Washington, DC: Congress of the U.S., Congressional Budget Office, 1984.

Zinsser, William K. *On Writing Well.* 5th ed. New York: HarperCollins, 1998.

———. *Writing to Learn.* New York: Harper and Row, 1988.

Resources on Accompanying Correspondence

Adams, Robert L., ed. *The Adams Cover Letter*. Holbrook, MA: Adams Publishing, 1995.

Asher, Donald. *The Overnight Job Change Letter*. Berkeley, CA: Ten Speed Press, 1994.

Beatty, Richard H. *175 High Impact Cover Letters*. New York: John Wiley & Sons, Inc., 2002.

Besson, Taunee. *Cover Letters*. New York: John Wiley & Sons, 1989.

Burgett, Gordon. *The Writer's Guide to Query Letters and Cover Letters*. Rocklin, CA: Prima Publishing, Inc., 1991.

Farr, Richard. *The Quick Resume and Cover Letter Book*. Indianapolis, IN: JIST Works, 1994.

Frank, William S. *200 Letters for Job Hunters*. Berkeley, CA: Ten Speed Press, 1993.

Hansen, Katherine, and Randall Hansen. *Dynamic Cover Letters: How to Write the Letter That Gets You the Job*. Berkeley, CA: Ten Speed Press, 2001.

Kaplan, Bonnie Miller. *Sure-Hire Cover Letters*. New York: American Management Association, 1994.

Krannich, Ronald L., and Caryl Rae Krannich. *Dynamic Cover Letters and Other Great Job Search Letters*. Manassas Park, VA: Impact Publications, 1998.

————. *The Perfect Cover Letter*. New York: John Wiley & Sons, 1997.

Krannich, Ronald L., and William J. Banis. *High Impact Resumes and Letters*. 6th ed. Manassas, VA: Impact Publications, 2002.

Marler, Patty, and Jan Bailey Mattia. *Cover Letters Made Easy*. Lincolnwood, IL: VGM Career Horizons, 1996.

Martin, Eric R., and Karyn E. Langhorne. *How to Write Successful Cover Letters*. Lincolnwood, IL: VGM Horizons, 1994.

Neal, James E., and Dorothy J. Neal. *Effective Letters for Business, Professional and Personal Use*. Perrysburg, OH: Neal Publications, Inc., 1999.

Provenzano, Steven. *Top Secret Resumes and Cover Letters*. Dearborn, MI: Financial Publishing, Inc., 1996.

Wynett, Stanley. *Cover Letters That Will Get You the Job You Want*. Cincinnati: Better Way Books, 1993.

About the Authors

Acy L. Jackson is president of Acy L. Jackson & Associates, which provides career, interpersonal, and intercultural consultation services for private sector employers and educational institutions. He was associate dean of students and director of the Career Planning Center at Colgate University in Hamilton, New York. In those capacities he counseled students and young professionals who applied to graduate and professional schools, sought employment, and/or applied for graduate fellowships. He was also a part-time instructor at the English Language Institute at Syracuse University.

Prior to Colgate, Jackson was associate dean of students, director of the career planning and placement center, and instructor-at-large at the College of Wooster in Ohio. He has also been director of Armaghan English Language Institute in Tehran, Iran, and has taught English at a boarding school in West Pakistan.

Jackson holds a B.B.A. from Westminster College (PA), an M.Ed. from the University of Pittsburgh, and an M.A. from Teachers College, Columbia University. Selected as a participant in the Institute for Educational Management at Harvard University in 1985, he received the Administrative Development Award from Colgate University that year. He has served as distinguished instructor of career life planning for the American Management Association's Operation Enterprise Program.

Jackson has published articles on teaching English as a foreign language and career planning for undergraduates. In the fall of 1989, he was one of three Americans selected to participate in an international seminar on career planning and placement at the University of Oxford in England.

Since 1997, Jackson has taught writing at Terra Community College and Owens Community College in Ohio.

C. Kathleen Geckeis lived in Germany and studied German, art history, and British and American literature at the Universität des Saarlandes from 1977 to 1986. As methodology instructor at the Berlitz School of Languages in Saarbrücken, Saarland, she taught English as a Foreign Language, as well as Business English to corporations, such as Mannesmag Demag and the Deutsche Bank, from 1980 to 1986.

In 1988, Geckeis received a B.A. in German Language, Literature, and Translation, *cum laude*. At the top of the class, she was first to receive an M.A. in German Translation and Literature from the Applied Linguistics Institute at Kent State University.

In 1997, Geckeis earned an M.A. in English from the University of Toledo. A ten-year veteran of community college education, she has taught and developed a variety of courses, including Elementary and Intermediate German, Composition I and II, Technical Report Writing, Business Communication, the American Novel, Short Fiction, Introduction to Humanities, Critical Thinking, Business for International Trade, and Developmental Reading and Writing. Geckeis has also worked as a freelance interpreter and as an in-house translator.

Since 2000, Geckeis has been the Manager of the Writing Center at Owens Community College. In the spring of 2002, Geckeis presented a paper at the International Writing Centers Association Conference in Savannah, GA.